"Whether you're a sales person or a sai~ ~~~~~, your time is too valuable to read another sales book that tells you what you already know. *NeuroSelling®* is very different. It will fundamentally change the way you think about selling and if you apply the *NeuroSelling®* process, it will dramatically improve your results."

—MATT RIEBEL, CHIEF SALES OFFICER, PROTECTIVE LIFE

"This isn't just another book on mastering sales acumen. *NeuroSelling®* is a real-world guide on building trust, strengthening relationships and driving genuine and intelligent sales conversations."

—BRAD LARSEN, SENIOR DIRECTOR,
BUSINESS DEVELOPMENT, MITSUBISHI ELECTRIC

"Understanding your customer, how they think and what motivates them to say 'yes' to your sales team is about more than just a relationship—it's an artful science that Jeff explains with masterful simplicity. His insights, experience and methodology in *NeuroSelling®* is a pathway to profitability and should be required reading for any team serious about excelling in today's dynamic marketplace."

—JIM PEARSON, CEO, NICO CORPORATION

"This book goes straight to the heart of why traditional sales techniques don't give us the results we want. Then it provides a systematic, scientifically proven path from the inside out; a true people-first approach. Thanks, Jeff, for showing us a better way!"

—NORA STEWART, CEO, ENTHEOS

"Finally! A sales book that dismantles all of the 'slimy' sales gimmicks of old and addresses the heart and science of a purposeful and successful sales conversation. Do not engage another customer until you have read this book."

—TOMMY SEAY, DIRECTOR, BUSINESS DEVELOPMENT, AMERICAN EXPRESS

"It's rare to find someone who understands the art AND science of sales so well. Jeff Bloomfield is at the top of the list!"

—EDDIE YOUNG, SR. VICE PRESIDENT, SALES, FRESHPET

"I am a skeptic by nature. I put half my sales team through *NeuroSelling®* and the other half did things the old way. The result? The *NeuroSelling®* group increased sales by 35% over their peers. Naturally, everyone got the book after that! Jeff is a master communicator. This is the most effective methodology I have ever seen!"

—ANDREW WYANT, PRESIDENT, ISSA

"*NeuroSelling®* provides an understanding into the science behind customer decision making and provides a road map to master it. Most sales books are either too theoretical, too basic or another version of a similar methodology but with a different acronym. *NeuroSelling®* is a fantastic balance of 'why' and 'how.' The book is in and of itself, self-evident, as the stories in it compel you to read on. I highly recommend reading it and applying its learnings!"

—CHAD BRINES, VICE PRESIDENT, SALES, OCULAR THERAPEUTICS

"As a CEO, I was engaged from the first page! I found this content so relatable and applicable. I really eat this type of knowledge up. Jeff's insight into more impactful communication will continue to help me refine my skills as a leader. Bravo!"

—JARROD MCCARROLL, CEO, WEBER, INC.

"Understanding the science behind customer decision making and having a road map to master it? Brilliant."

—DAVE NURRE, REGIONAL PRESIDENT, USI INSURANCE

"Jeff teaches you how to build trust faster and drive change through customer conversation with a unique and science-based approach. He is a product of his product in that, he gives the lessons by using the very concepts to train you on their value! This is a must-read for any sales professional. With *NeuroSelling®,* Jeff helps you develop the skills and principles necessary for anyone to build a more satisfying and fulfilling sales career."

—Tom Ziglar, CEO, Ziglar, Inc.

"A must read if your sales target is a living, breathing, thinking human being! These principles seem so obvious after reading the book, but how many sales reps actually use them in their day to day? Great read, it will change the way you sell!"

—Joe Schowalter, Global Marketing Director, Ethicon, Inc.

"Jeff is a master communicator and this book explains why! A must read for your sales team, and anyone wanting to improve their connections with people—*NeuroSelling®* is the perfect balance of 'why' and 'how'."

—Caitlin Clipp, Executive Director, United Healthcare

"I've worked with clients in the Fortune 100 who haven't discovered what Jeff Bloomfield has taught for years: B2B sales success is a system. In *NeuroSelling®,* Jeff provides a working understanding of the science behind sales, then shows how to use it to positively nail that first critical customer conversation. I expect to see his book soon on executives' desks everywhere."

—Matthew Pollard, Author of *The Introvert's Edge: How the Quiet and Shy Can Outsell Anyone*

NEURO
SELLING

Mastering the Customer Conversation
Using the Surprising Science of Decision-Making

JEFF BLOOMFIELD

 Axon Publishing

*"The first and simplest emotion
which we discover in the human mind, is curiosity."*

—EDMUND BURKE (1729–1797), IRISH STATESMAN,
AUTHOR, AND PHILOSOPHER

CONTENTS

WHY THEY BUY (AND WHEN THEY DON'T)

"The really important question is this:
Why would a person do business with you at all?"
—ROY H. WILLIAMS, *THE WIZARD OF ADS*

MY SON, DREW, has a life-threatening allergy. Ingesting the smallest amount—or simply being exposed to peanuts—can trigger anaphylaxis. It can be deadly for him, depending on how much he's exposed to and how long it takes to treat it with epinephrine.

Our family has epi pens stashed everywhere. Drew's backpack, my wife's purse, sling pack, cargo shorts pockets, vehicles, at home, at church, Drew's taekwondo bag—anywhere we're going to be, there's going to an epi pen within reach.

Before the beginning of every school year, we meet with Drew's teachers and school staff to emphasize the severity of his allergy and review their plan for keeping our son safe and healthy. Year after year since kindergarten, we would begin the frustrating ritual of scheduling the meeting with his school staff and administrators. We had struggled through kindergarten, then first grade, followed by second, and each year it became more and more frustrating at the seemingly passive, almost dismissive attitude we received from the school staff. In our eyes, it was as if they didn't really view this as a problem at all. Meanwhile, we were seeing article after article of mourning parents whose child died from unnecessary peanut exposure due to surroundings (including schools) that didn't have the necessary protection in place for their child.

For the beginning of his third-grade year, we walked into the room where the teachers and principal had assembled for our yearly ritual. Once again, we could see that the teachers and staff were not viewing this as importantly as we knew the problem to be. New year, same perceived lack of urgency. From their perspective, I'm sure they felt they were used to dealing with parents whose children had food allergies, that this was a run-of-the-mill conversation for them. They were nice and attentive, but their focus seemed to be on reassuring us, the scared parents, that they saw this kind of thing all the time and would take care of Drew "just like we have all the other students who've come through our school."

My wife went through her annual presentation of all the signs and symptoms of anaphylaxis with all the supporting facts and data to support the need for urgent attention and action. The response was the usual, "Yep. We got it." "We will make sure none of the kids with peanut butter or peanut products gives any to Drew." "We will do our best to be sure he doesn't eat the wrong thing, etc.... etc.... etc...." I was frustrated. Hazel was close to tears. We weren't exaggerating or being dramatic when we said "life-threatening." These teachers just saw two scared parents. We saw a group of people who we believed didn't understand how serious Drew's allergy was. In other words, they didn't see a problem. They were just dealing with nervous parents; we were fighting for our son's life.

We needed them to change. We needed them to see the need to move from their current "status quo" to a place that was actually mutually beneficial for both parties.

What could we do to get them to get it? To really, truly *get it?*

Apparently at an impasse, we all fell silent for a moment while we gathered our thoughts and tried to figure out a way forward. I was racking my brain and trying my best to suppress the stress and frustration I could feel coursing through my veins. I help people communicate with prospects in a way that drives urgency to change every day! Yet I was momentarily stuck. My way forward in this moment was likely to include a scorched-earth communication approach but I was fervently holding my tongue. With tears in her eyes, my insightful and wisdom-filled wife, Hazel, looked up from the undersized elementary school table and quietly asked, "Would any one of you let a student bring a loaded gun to school?"

Immediate confusion. I could almost read the teachers' thoughts: *Wha-huh? Weren't we just talking about peanut butter?!*

Hazel pressed on: "Every time you let a student bring anything made from peanuts into the classroom, it's the same as if they're pointing a loaded gun at Drew. That's how dangerous his allergy is."

Yes, I understand that in today's culture, using a gun analogy, particularly in a classroom setting, may make some of you a tad bit uncomfortable. But you have to know my wife. She is humble and kind. She is naturally a reserved person who isn't prone to emotional language or hyperbole. In addition, she was a former educator and everyone in that room knew her and trusted her. As those words rolled from her lips, in that one moment, something shifted. Something changed.

All the information and conversation up to that point appeared to finally click. The attitude of everyone in the room went from politely patronizing a couple of overprotective parents to complete buy-in and cooperation. They finally connected with our message. They finally had an urgency to change. They had a different perspective on the problem.

Whether you realize it or not, the issues we faced in that elementary classroom sitting on those multicolored chairs a couple of sizes too small for adults is exactly the same thing you face in your day-to-day sales conversations.

> Every day, you're trying to influence people to make different decisions than the ones they have been making. To influence their behavior. To increase their urgency. To induce change. Understanding what drives human behavior and decision-making from a scientific standpoint...that's what NeuroSelling® is all about.

The Great Disconnect—Why Your Message May Miss the Mark

Why wasn't providing the teachers and administrators the information, the facts, the data and signs and symptoms around Drew's life-threatening allergy enough? What was it that my wife said that finally clicked for everyone in that room?

The epiphany certainly didn't come from Hazel's tears or my obvious frustration. Schools deal with tearful moms and angry dads just like us all the time. While our educators are not unfeeling robots, after so many meetings with unhappy parents, they have to become thick-skinned during these types of meetings just to keep their own sanity. We weren't dealing with uncaring drones—we just couldn't get past the professional outer shell they'd created after so many meetings with helicopter parents who really did overreact to every minor issue, and quite honestly, they felt they had the answers, knew enough, and didn't need further "convincing" to change their actions or behaviors.

And aren't your customers the same way?

When our clients' salespeople snag a few minutes of their customer's time, be it a surgeon standing outside the operating room, an engineer in his office, or walk into a conference room to pitch to the customer's executive team, they face the same situation Hazel and I did—a roomful of people who already have their guard up, who already assume they know what the salesperson is going to say, and who already believe they are likely doing things well enough to not need whatever they're selling.

You know how this scene plays out, don't you?

Here's the frustrating thing: You know with certainty that your product is superior to the competition's. If you're like most of our clients, you probably charge a premium of 20 percent or more over the competition because of how superior your product or service is.

Despite you knowing that and even stating that...the person on the other side of this conversation has heard it all before. Every salesperson claims to have the best, be the best, and care the best. Every one of them. They see you as just another anonymous parent—excuse me, sales rep—singing the same tune they've heard so many times.

You know you're different.

But how can you get them to *get it?*

Hazel uttered three sentences that changed the entire feel of the room and transformed those educators into partners and guardians of our child. I felt elated. But when I later replayed the scene in my head, I could have smacked myself. Of course what she did worked—in a microcosm, it was exactly how we teach people to successfully sell every day! They trusted her personally (connection), they believed she knew her stuff (credibility) so, in the end, she just needed to find a way to put their current thinking (status quo) at risk. And that she did. When your customers trust you personally and they see you know your stuff professionally, you can begin to communicate in a way that naturally forces them to see things from a different perspective and create urgency to solve problems that they either didn't know they had or may be trying to solve ineffectively. This book will be your road map to help you do exactly that.

After working in and around biotech for a couple of decades, and then as a consultant for a number of neuroscience-related companies, I've had the good fortune and access to scores of data and research on how the human brain works. While much of it is still a mystery to medical science, here is what we do know:

> How we behave and make decisions are driven not just by psychology, but biology and physiology. Understanding how all three of these elements work in concert to process information to either resist or choose change is the secret sauce behind the impact every great communicator exhibits, whether they realize it or not.

You intuitively know this. You know that when you're feeling anxious or angry, you make different decisions than you would when you feel calm, cool, and collected. (Don't ever go to the grocery store hungry—you'll come home with enough food to open your own store!)

You and I might like to believe that, in a B2B (Business to Business) setting, we make more reasonable and rational decisions than we would as a typical consumer. The truth is our neurochemistry works the same way, regardless of where we are. We likely won't make an impulse buy of an enterprise software platform, of course, but the way our brains work still governs how we eventually arrive at our decisions, even when the buying cycle spans months or even years.

After digging into the neuroscience behind customer decision-making (really, human decision-making in general) and validating what we've found with the success of thousands of sales reps we've trained and coached, leaders we've mentored, and companies we've consulted with from the small to the Fortune 100, I can confidently tell you why the traditional approach to customer conversations is so ineffective.

Before we venture too deeply into the realm of neuroscience-based communication, let me ask you this: Have you ever stopped to ask yourself how you learned to communicate the way you do? Some of it may have come from your education and training, but my guess is a great deal of it came from your roots. The best communicators do so from a place of "why" vs. "what" and they know where their "why" came from.

I can tell you exactly where mine came from. The farm. And one of my earliest teachers? Papaw Willie Bloomfield.

Why Before What

I'm an old farm boy from north central Ohio. My grandfather—"Papaw"—bought a farm of nearly a hundred acres with his life savings when my dad was just a boy, having moved the family up from Kentucky. With just an eighth-grade education, he was the smartest man I'd ever met. He was an amazing storyteller and communicator.

He taught me how to drive when I was just five years old, standing between his knees on our old, green, John Deere tractor. He believed hard work and perseverance will get you everywhere you need to go in life. He believed that problem-solvers rule the world. That with enough ingenuity, creativity, and—in our case—maybe a little bit of duct tape, you could solve almost any problem.

He also taught me what I call today the Platinum Rule: *You should treat other people better than they expect to be treated and it'll always come back to you.*

And whether he was borrowing old man Crouse's red truck from down the road that seemed to frequently be on empty and returning it full of gas, or giving his coat off his back, literally, to an older man during a farm sale in the dead of winter, that's just how Papaw lived his life.

The last thing he taught me was that family matters more than anything else. And long after our work colleagues and friends are gone, your family remains—so you've got to treat them accordingly along the journey. Papaw came from a long line of storytellers. He could weave a tale like

Shakespeare himself, be it about his latest fishing trip or simply to make a point about why we were moving the cattle from one field to the other. People seemed to love listening to him...most of all, me.

On a cold February day in 1982, I jumped off the school bus to head down his fifty-yard-long driveway like I did nearly every day before. Instead of seeing just his green Chevy Silverado parked at the end, on this day, it was full of cars. Not too long after, an ambulance came screaming down our snow-covered dirt road and down that same fifty-yard-long driveway.

Unfortunately for me, he had stage 4 lung cancer and that would be the last day I would ever see him again. I was devastated to lose my mentor, my hero. But what he really taught me was how to take those beliefs and apply them in a way that is meaningful to someone else. To make a difference in the world and in the lives of others. And my Papaw, being a great storyteller, great communicator, and influencer, essentially taught me this methodology long before I was able to validate it with actual science. Thanks in large part to him, I'm able to take these concepts and beliefs and turn them into something that you can hopefully use to make yourself even more effective in the way you communicate... be it as a salesperson, a leader, a parent, or the coach of your kid's little league team. And that's what NeuroSelling was born out of. In a lot of ways, I owe a great deal of my company and my life today to my Papaw. And that's really why I do what I do.

With that as the backdrop, what I found anecdotally over the course of my career as well as pouring over the volumes of published research on the topics of neuroscience and human behavior is that much of what *prevents* us from communicating like Papaw may not be your fault.

You've been trained to sell backward.

Neuroscience and Sales: What's in the Mind Is All That Matters

When you were hired, how much of your company's training was devoted to understanding how to build trust faster...creating deep and lasting empathetic connections with your customers? I'll bet none. In fact, I've asked a number of CEOs and sales VPs how much training is devoted to interpersonal skills and communication. You know what I hear more often than not? "They're supposed to already know how to do that stuff. That's their job."

Instead, they keep pouring budget into new technology, different sales systems, more data, and failed "sales training du jour," while ignoring the most crucial and yet most overlooked part of a sales/customer relationship: successfully communicating with the customer in a way that builds trust faster and creates urgency to change.

Let me know if this sounds at all familiar:

On your first day, you were probably handed a binder chock-full of product specifications, data, research, facts, and figures along with a binder of policies and procedures. You were assigned an area or territory to cover. You probably spent two weeks or more going through online eLearning modules and maybe a couple of months shadowing senior sales reps, followed by a few days of in-person "sales training" then told to get out there and hustle. We refer to this as the "rep" factory. Every company has a version of this and, in the end, it tends to spit out the same product (you) with a different label (your brand).

You know the facts, data, features, and benefits cold.

Then, when you want to up your game, you typically turn to sales books or conventional sales "trainers," and inevitably work on refining your sales tactics—i.e. rapport building, body language, mirroring body language, closing "ABCs," social proof, the law of reciprocity, asking probing questions, etc.

Sales tactics? Check. You have those in abundance.

And for a time, many executives thought (and hoped) technology might hold the secret, so they invested heavily in sales software. They found out that tech is a great enabler and potential sales multiplier tool, but it's only as good as its users. Likely, your company has rolled out programs that infuse marketing into the sales process, leveraging the latest and greatest systems and processes.

Tech? Check.

But let's go back to basics for a moment.

Effective selling really begins and ends with the customer conversation, doesn't it? This is the true "moment of impact."

I hate to be the first person you may hear this from, but what if I told you your fundamental approach to communicating may be wrong? You were trained to present facts and data...features and benefits, armed with sales tactics and an entire support team behind you. In short, you've done everything you can do to ready yourself to win the customer.

> But no one trained you on how the human brain makes decisions, which leaves you at a significant disadvantage with most salespeople communicating the wrong information at the wrong time and in the wrong order.

We will dive into this in much more detail in later chapters but when we think of the brain, we usually picture the two lobes of gray matter. That's a brain, right? Well, it is and it isn't. You might find it easier to think of the brain as three brains, all working together to keep you and me alive and well.

Science-Powered Sales Conversations

The two-lobed gray matter you're thinking of is our neocortex, responsible for our higher reasoning. That's where our self-awareness and conscious thought happens. It's what you're using right now to read this book and judge its validity. It's literally how we "think"; therefore we refer to this area as our "thinking" brain.

But the other two parts of the brain hold more sway over our actions and behaviors: the limbic system (made up of areas like the amygdala and hippocampus), which we call the "feeling" brain and what I simply call the root brain, our "instinctive brain" (comprising the brainstem, basal ganglia, and other elements). These two "subbrains" essentially run in the background, in our subconscious. You don't have to think about making your heart beat. I don't need to think about yanking my hand away from a hot stove. Hazel didn't consciously decide to tear up in those moments with the school staff. Our limbic and root brains take care of those types of instinctive and emotional reactions without us needing to consciously think about them.

More importantly for the purpose of this book, **the limbic and root brains initially *override* our neocortex.**

I could be in the middle of an important phone call, but if a car backfires in front of my office, my subconscious immediately overrides my conscious and points my attention to the source of the loud sound. Only after I know that there's no threat can I turn my attention back to my phone conversation. As famed researcher and neurobiologist Joseph LeDoux states in his commentary on the study of emotion:

> *Our studies have led us to understand that the amygdala is the key, no matter how the stimulus comes into the brain: through the eyes, the nose, the ears. The amygdala is programmed to react without benefit of input from the thinking part of the brain, the cortex. Eventually the cortex gets involved, but this processing takes longer.*[1]

You don't need to memorize the parts of the brain to understand the big takeaway here:

Human decision-making *starts* by processing information in the limbic and root brains and is then *validated* by the neocortex.

While we might believe that our decision-making begins in our neocortex (where we become consciously aware of our thoughts), the science you're going to read about in this book shows that it's actually the opposite. Like an iceberg, most of the brain's activity happens below the surface.[2] Our decision-making process starts with the instinctive and emotional filters of our subconscious, then gets passed up to our rational, conscious mind to affirm, validate, or reject that information.

In short, we buy on emotion and justify with logic.

A few years back, we had a gentleman in one of our workshops who challenged the idea that we make decisions emotionally and subconsciously, then use our rational mind to validate the emotional decision. He gave me the example of his recent bike purchase. He's an avid cyclist and wanted to upgrade his gear. He combed through all the data on different bikes available, even going so far as to make a spreadsheet with all the specs. He then made his purchase: a pro bike for almost $3,000. He was adamant about the fact that he had made a rational, conscious decision. No emotion there.

"That's great," I said. "So, you're a hard-core cyclist, huh?"

"Aww yeah, man. Every weekend. I bike for miles in some of the most gorgeous places you've ever seen."

"I bet! So, what is it about cycling that you like so much?" I asked.

He got this dreamy look on his face as he began talking about it: "I love it. The freedom, the peace, the road, the connection, and the sense of calm I feel. Seeing the world in a whole different way than you do behind a windshield at sixty or seventy miles-an-hour."

After he trailed off, I said, "Can I point something out? Everything you've just described is based on emotion. Or as you called it, irrational emotion. If you simply wanted to exercise, you could buy an exercise bike. No chance of getting hit by a car in your living room. If you simply wanted a bicycle to leisurely ride around and take in the beautiful sites, you can find one at a garage sale for a lot less than $3,000. But you wanted to enhance the emotional experience you get from cycling through the mountains. Cycling isn't about what you do, it's about who you are. It sounds to me like you'd already made an emotional decision to buy a top-of-the-line bike. After that, it was simply a question of which one. You had chosen an expensive bike well before you even began your evaluation. Your 'logical' evaluation was simply an exercise in justifying spending that much money on a bike."

His fellow trainees began laughing as a confused look came across his face. He still wanted to argue that he didn't make emotional decisions, but everyone else in the room saw the truth, plain as day. By the end of the course, he was *feeling* that way too.

Why do we believe our customers are any different?

When you're in a sales conversation, you've been trained to present information to your customer's rational, reasoning neocortex: facts and figures, features and benefits. You're trying to get them to make a decision by appealing to the most recalcitrant, least persuaded, and least impactful decision-making part of the brain.

That's why we hit a stalemate in the conversation with Drew's teachers. Hazel and I had been presenting facts, informing them of his condition. Their neocortices filtered everything we said and silently explained away our concerns, as they already understood all they needed to know *about* the issue and had no compelling emotional reason to act or behave differently. In other words, there was no problem; therefore no need for a solution. We could see in their faces and their language that they weren't going to substantially change anything. They weren't going to treat Drew any different than any of the other allergy sufferers who'd passed through the hallowed halls of their prestigious learning institution. They weren't going to treat Hazel and me any differently than any of the other helicopter parents who'd demanded their child be given special treatment.

These were genuinely good people who just weren't connecting with what we were saying. Their neocortex said, *We've already heard all this before. We've had plenty of kids with allergies and we've always taken care of them. Let's reassure these two parents and get out of here—school opens tomorrow and we've got a million things left to do!*

What Hazel intuitively did was brilliant. (I'd like to pretend that she's picked up something from hearing me talk about this stuff all the time, but she was that kind of smart way before we ever met.) She used a "neural" pattern interrupter to disengage their neocortex and spike the cortisol, activating the emotional centers of their limbic and root brains. Embedded in that pattern interrupter "story" was an immediate, fear-inducing visual antagonist: a loaded gun endangering a helpless student. Was it an over-the-top analogy? Maybe, but when you are up against status quo, sometimes you have to take drastic visual, emotional measures. She then created a new synaptic connection between the image and the associated emotions of a loaded gun to those seemingly innocent enough peanuts.

Once that new neural pathway was established, the root and limbic brains then overrode the neocortex's old reasoning. Instead of seeing two overconcerned parents, their neocortex followed the limbic and root brains' direction, which said, "Here are two people trying to save their son from real danger!" It changed everything. It might even have saved Drew's life.

Moment of Impact: Fifteen Minutes of Life or Death

"Jeff, I have to confess: I fully buy into NeuroSelling, but I'm nervous about introducing it at my company. We have in the neighborhood of a million dollars invested in another sales 'system' and I'm...well, I guess I just don't want people to get confused."

I recognized what he really meant. This CEO was nervous bringing in another sales "program" and running the risk of muddying the waters. Even though they really weren't getting the results they needed, he didn't want to say that he'd potentially made a bad decision with another sales system, especially after investing that kind of money.

"I completely understand," I said, "but NeuroSelling is not a sales system. It's actually a communication methodology. It's about having effective conversations with your customers that build trust faster and drives urgency to change based on the science of human decision-making."

He looked a little confused, which is what I'd hoped for: I'd piqued his attention.

"Let me explain. You sell medical devices, right? What does it look like when your salespeople pitch to a surgeon? Are they sitting in a nice, quiet conference room with a sleek PowerPoint and the surgeon's full attention?"

"I wish!" he laughed.

"Right. Most of the time, they have fifteen minutes—and, really, more like five—between surgeries. The salesperson and the surgeon are standing in a hospital hallway, the doctor is just coming out of one surgery and getting ready to go into another, nurses are running between rooms, lights are flashing, alarms beeping and buzzing, life and death happening all around them, the surgeon's mind is still on their last patient, this is their third sales rep interaction of the day, and your salesperson has just fifteen minutes—and really five—to completely capture their attention."

I gave him a moment to paint that picture in his mind. "If that conversation doesn't go anywhere, if it doesn't captivate the doctor, if it doesn't lead to any action, *nothing else matters*. Everything in your company hinges on those fifteen minutes. If you want higher sales, if you want to grow your company, if you want to save more lives with your medical devices, then everything you do has to focus on supporting *that* conversation in that hallway, one-on-one with that doctor. Until that domino falls, nothing else matters. Now, let me ask you this: How do they sell today?"

"Well, they're armed with the data from the clinical trials and—"

"Right there," I stopped him. "Right there: you're talking about facts and figures, features and benefits: why your device is better than what they're using right now. And it is! I've read the data from your clinical trials. It absolutely is. But when you start talking about why your tech is superior to what they've been doing, you've fallen into the trap the majority of businesses fall into: attempting to sell to the wrong part of the brain. I continued, "In fact, they aren't just speaking to the wrong part of the surgeon's brain, they are doing so in a way that causes the surgeon to resist! Essentially, at a subconscious level, they are telling them that what they've been doing is wrong and that they must be some sort of idiot! We human beings like to think of ourselves as pretty good decision makers. When you layer on a human being who is an educated professional at their position, well, let's just say that person likely feels they know a heck of a lot more than you do. And now you're going to tell me that I've been wrong all this time? Probably not the best way to drive change, huh?"

This CEO didn't need a better sales system; his salespeople just needed to have better problem-solving sales conversations.

Unfortunately, he'd fallen into the same boat as nearly every other company: training on the "hard" stuff (facts and data), assuming too much on the "soft stuff" and having no way to ensure the order in which the conversation took place incentivized change instead of inciting resistance. **But whether you sell medical devices, life insurance, elevators, or envelopes, companies live or die according to what happens in those "moment of impact" customer meetings.**

So why don't we train our salespeople on how to have incredibly effective conversations?

Every salesperson is trained on coming across with professional credibility. On one hand, that makes sense. It's hard to sell premium engineered machinery, enterprise SaaS, or medical devices if you have no idea what you're talking about, right? But sales organizations almost never train salespeople on how to build trust the right way and in the right order in a way that creates meaningful connection *and* drives urgency to change.

So regardless of how many VPs of sales tell me, "I hire good, experienced people—they're already supposed to know how to do that stuff. We just train them on our particular product," it doesn't change the fact that this approach simply isn't enough.

Unfortunately, their salespeople came from other companies that assumed the same thing. When were you trained and coached on how to build genuine trust and establish a real human connection? You weren't. And what does your new employer train you on? The exact opposite: facts and figures, features, and benefits. You know how to establish professional credibility on the products and services you offer, but not until someone trusts you personally will their brain allow them to be open to how you may help them professionally. Until you get their stress level down and their feelings of trust and safety up (more on neurochemistry later), he or she won't allow themselves to believe that you're not there simply on your own agenda. Yes, the most important part of the entire sales process—the thing that the *entire* business hinges on—is what happens in that meeting. No pressure, huh?

Everything in your company, from payroll to R&D to overhead, all rests on what happens in the conversation you and your peers have with the customer and your ability to motivate them to give you money in exchange for your product or service. If that's the most important thing, doesn't it make sense that, above all else, you become an expert at the customer conversation?

It's time to move beyond the traditional, transactional sales rep training "factory" model and move into a new age of communication that is grounded in science and allows you to be authentic, genuine, and yet still drive the conversation in a way that creates urgency to change.

NeuroSelling: A New Communication Model

NeuroSelling will equip you with a working knowledge of the biology, psychology, and physiology of human decision-making so that you can have more effective, and impactful customer conversations. As a professional communicator, you need an understanding of how the human brain works so that you're working with the human mind, not against it.

Let me state what NeuroSelling and the rest of this book *are not:*

- ⊗ a new spin on old, traditional selling models

- ⊗ another sales "system"

- ⊗ just another sales process

This *communication* model/methodology doesn't need to displace or replace whatever you're doing now. Think of it this way: if your current sales process or sales model were a racecar, NeuroSelling isn't a replacement for that vehicle. It's the rocket fuel to help you win more races. It's a way to shortcut the meetings that lead to nowhere, the months of establishing credibility, the multiple phone calls and meetings that lead to yet more meetings, and sales cycles that last far too long.

I'm going to give you a working knowledge—only what you need to know—about how to lead a sales conversation by speaking to the areas of the brain that really make all the decisions. You're going to experience the powerful advantage of using strategic narratives to engage your customers on an emotional, subconscious level that builds trust and drives change.

Wouldn't it be great if you understood exactly what your customer is thinking at all times?

Wouldn't it be fantastic if you knew the process that they go through in their mind in order to make a decision?

What is decision-making after all?

It's simply the mental process that a person, including your customer, goes through in order to choose between multiple options. Between option A or option B, even if one of those options is status quo—doing nothing different. So how do our customers *choose?*

How do you choose? It's all built in and hard-wired into our brains. There's a science behind the way every human being makes a decision, yes, including your customers. And when you understand that process, you understand the biology that our brains use and go through to make decisions, what happens as a sales and marketing professional is you can start to craft a more compelling and influential message that hits the part of your customer's brain where they're more receptive and less antagonistic to your message.

We will break the rest of the book into two sections. Part 1: The Lab is all the foundational science and research you need to understand "why" we must communicate differently. Part 2: The Field is your practical road map to implement NeuroSelling directly into your customer conversations. Do yourself a favor, overachiever and don't skip Part 1. Trust me. It's the very information your brain will need to justify moving from your current sales safety box and into a new realm of influence.

I've been fortunate enough to share this NeuroSelling methodology with thousands upon thousands of salespeople all over the world. I've seen how it's changed not only their careers but also their lives. I sincerely hope you experience the same over your journey through this book.

That journey starts next with learning in Part 1: The Lab.

For Access to Free Bonus Tools to Help You Implement
the Concepts of NeuroSelling, go to:

www.braintrustgrowth.com/neurosellingtools

PART I

THE LAB

SELLING VS. *NEUROSELLING*

*"We are not in the coffee business serving people,
but the people business serving coffee."*
—HOWARD SCHULTZ, CEO OF STARBUCKS

THE VICE PRESIDENT of sales for a large B2B software company got up on stage. Behind him, the two massive, thirty-by-fifty screens displayed the tech company's year-to-date and year-over-year sales revenue. In front of him was the company's salesforce of several hundred people. I sat in the very back of the hotel ballroom, waiting for my turn on stage as this year's keynote speaker.

John looked like the stereotypical vice president of sales from central casting—tall, fit, and confident, yet relaxed and charismatic. As he began to give his talk, I could see why he'd been successful and risen to the level he did.

He began by showing the usual columns and pie charts representing the sales figures for each of the last three quarters, then showed the gap between that and their annual sales goal. He broke down how much each sales team needed to sell in the fourth quarter to hit the goal. His next few slides of bullet points laid out the types of business clients they were targeting, average closing ratios, and new product specifications and features to use in sales presentations. All in all, the typical corporate sales talk.

Now, I'm not sure if you're aware of this or not, but a roomful of salespeople is a pretty hard audience to keep engaged. You've heard the old phrase, "The mind can only absorb what the butt can endure," right? The longer John talked, the more people began fidgeting in their seats, checking their phones, and whispering to their coworkers beside them. Toward the back where John couldn't see them, I even saw some on Facebook and playing Candy Crush.

He wrapped up his talk with the typical Knute Rockne rallying cry of "Okay, let's get out there and crush Q4!" Everyone provided the customary polite golf clap. (Of course they did; wouldn't you applaud your boss's boss's boss?)

Then John introduced the next speaker, scheduled to go on just before me. "Alright, now Christina Yearwood" (not her real name, so don't go googling her) from corporate HR is coming up to talk about our leadership development program."

The thirty-something woman who bounded up on stage was as excited as she was nervous. She thanked the VP, but then fumbled a little in her lead-in. After a minute or two, she began to find her rhythm and then launched into a sales pitch encouraging people in the room to join the program. She quickly related a few success stories and then singled out a couple of people in the room who'd already signed up. It sounded like a solid program and I saw more than one head in the room nodding along.

Then Christina played a video of testimonials from other people around the company who'd gone through the training. It seems like I've sat through a million of these, so I thought I knew what to expect, but I was pleasantly surprised. Instead of the usual generic praise, the people on screen were relating some personal and emotional experiences they'd had while going through this particular leadership development program and how it had impacted them as much on a personal discovery level as it did professionally.

I thought, *That's pretty cool.* Most companies don't go there. They like to keep things strictly business and don't encourage sharing too much personal information. The fact that this company had a leadership development course touting these types of experiences and benefits said a lot about how much they cared about their people as individuals.

Usually, this kind of pitch would end there. The person from corporate would wrap it up with directions on how to sign up and then thank the audience for their time. After that, it'd be my turn. I had already half stood up from my seat when Christina said, "My own personal journey through this program was one of amazing self-discovery and I'd like to share my story with you."

I thought, *Okay, this is different.* I sat back down in my chair and waited as she gathered her thoughts.

What happened in the next few minutes transformed what should have been a simple training pitch into an experience I doubt any of us in that ballroom will ever forget.

An Unscripted Experience of NeuroSelling

"When I was a child, I was the middle daughter of three girls. My father, however, had always wanted a boy. It seemed like every day he somehow found a way to remind us that we weren't what he wanted. He and my mother had tried three times and been disappointed every time. 'Three strikes and you're out,' he used to say to us. If we had been born boys, he'd say, he could take us to a ball game or work on cars together. But since we were girls, we weren't good for anything. The rest of the time, he just ignored us," Christina began.

"As the middle child, I felt especially neglected. I've learned now that experts call it 'middle child syndrome.' My oldest sister got most of my mother's attention because Mom depended on her so much; she was

'Mommy's little helper.' My youngest sister got attention because she was 'the baby' and we needed to 'watch out for her.' I just kind of got stuck in the middle."

Christina had to fight back some tears before continuing on.

"All my life, I felt like I was never good enough. I was so heartsick over being born a girl. 'If only I'd been born a boy,' I used to tell myself, 'my daddy would love me.' But it didn't matter how hard I tried or what I did, it was never enough. I grew up being ashamed for just being alive—for just being who I was.

"When I was a freshman in college, my dad walked out on us. No calls, no emails, no texts. He just left. We were all devastated. I'd never really been close to my family anyway, but instead of pulling us together, Dad leaving somehow pushed us all further apart. There I was, hundreds of miles away from my family, my father had just walked out of our lives, and my mother and sisters became even more distant. I had never been so lonely and heartbroken in my entire life."

I had become so caught up in her story that I'd completely forgotten everyone else sitting there in the ballroom. I came back to earth for a moment and saw everyone in the room entranced, leaning forward in their seats, hanging on her every word. We could all picture Christina in her college dorm crying. We could feel her heartache.

Intellectually, I recognized what was happening. Christina's story had bypassed our neocortex, responsible for our higher-level thinking, rationalizing, and judgment. Instead, she had engaged our limbic systems and root brains, responsible for personal trust, empathy, personal relationships, and a lab's worth of neurochemicals like dopamine and oxytocin. Despite knowing the neuroscience behind what was happening; despite teaching people to work *with* how our brain is designed (instead of against it); despite having an entire business dedicated to neuroscience selling techniques; despite the professional in me recognizing exactly what was going on…there I sat, in the back of the room, eyes filling with tears along with Christina's and engrossed in her story like everyone else!

But Christina quickly drew me back into her narrative. She had paused for a moment, but then her entire body language changed, as if she were preparing for something. Her voice lowered as she dropped the mother of all bombs.

"That loneliness and heartbreak…I couldn't take it. I tried to kill myself."

The temperature of the entire room dropped several degrees. I heard people throughout the audience react, some sucking in their breath or letting slip an involuntary "Oh, my…"

Christina said, "The only reason I'm alive is because my roommate found me and rescued me in time. After getting out of the hospital, I went into recovery for suicide victims. Through my experience, I met a man passionate about suicide prevention, the man who eventually became my husband. He's passionate about it because he lost his own roommate to suicide in college. With his love and understanding, I went through therapy and fully recovered, and reentered the workforce seven years ago.

"But guys, let me tell you what this leadership development program did: It made me look inside myself. It held a mirror up to who I am, not only as a professional but also as a person. And you know what? It helped me realize how I'd always unconsciously seen myself—as unworthy. This program helped me find a vision of who I'd like to be. Because of those two realizations, I was finally able to let go of all that hurt. I let go of those feelings of inadequacy. It affirmed my self-worth. I found out that I didn't need to feel like I wasn't good enough or that I'd never fit in. It gave me the sense of self I'd always been missing without even knowing it. I discovered that I can write the rest of my life story however I want to."

She smiled a beautiful, dazzling smile and said, "And I found a new purpose in life. I want to help other people realize that they don't have to live with the identity they've carried all their life, that they can define their own self-worth and purpose. That everyone's been created in a unique way and for a unique purpose. They need to find it and walk in that purpose."

With a tear-streaked face, she closed with, "That's what this program did for me. I would love if you'd let it do something similar for you too. Thank you."

The room exploded.

People were on their feet, cheering. The applause was deafening. Many were freely crying. I have never seen a standing ovation before or since for a leadership program commercial. What an unforgettable moment.

John took back the mic and said, "Wow! What a story. And now for our speaker!"

I mean, come on! How do you follow something like that!?

The Science Behind the Perfect Pitch

Fortunately for me, I could not have had a better setup. It was like I had paid Christina to work her magic in preparation for what I was about to share. Unbeknown to them, my entire talk revolved around creating exactly that kind of magic in client sales conversations. For the next hour, we talked about how to use neuroscience to do intentionally what Christina had done intuitively (and, most likely, accidentally).

After the talk, I was having lunch in the adjoining ballroom with a group of those salespeople. Of course, they were talking about how moving Christina's story was and how intriguing it was to have a presentation straight afterward explaining the science behind the experience.

In between forkfuls of macaroni, I said to the whole table, "Let me ask you something: Do you remember the bullet points on slide number four of John's presentation?"

They all stopped for a minute while they racked their brains. Someone said, "I think it was something around how much more everybody's team has to sell. Right?"

"Okay," I said, "what else? Remember any of the other bullet points? Any of the numbers from his graphs and charts?"

After everyone kind of shrugged, I said, "Okay, how about the main takeaway?"

"He just, I guess...he just wants everyone to sell more? That we need to bridge the gap in Q4?" one ventured. "What's this pop quiz for?"

"Pause for a second. Let me ask you this: What do you remember of Christina's story?"

Everyone started chiming in all at once: her suicide attempt, her husband's roommate, she had two sisters, her mother doting on the baby, her roommate finding her in her dorm room, her awakening and walking in her purpose. All of them had near-perfect recall of her entire story.

"Now, what was meaningful from John's talk?" I asked.

Same answer as before: "That we need to sell more."

I said, "So two people pitched two business ideas to you guys this morning that required you to potentially 'change' or do something 'different.' One person was an experienced sales professional with years of sales training under his belt. He was selling you on the idea that you need to keep doing what you've been doing—just do it better. Right?

"The other professional," I continued, "doesn't have a sales background. In fact, she's from HR. She got up to sell you on the idea that you needed to do something completely new and different—something that would make you uncomfortable, force you to change, and challenge your beliefs about yourself. Now, contrast those two sales pitches. Which one were you actually sold on?"

I mean, there wasn't a question. It wasn't even a contest. Christina's.

"Last question," I said. "Think about yourself in sales conversations in front of your customers. Which talk looks like what you do? John's? Or Christina's?"

Again, no question: definitely John's.

Smiling, I said, "You see the problem, right? You were convinced to change by Christina, but you sell like John!"

Conducting Your Sales Conversations in the Right Order

It's not their fault, though. Corporate sales training mostly consists of equipping the salesperson with facts and figures. When I was selling life-saving oncology drugs, I was taught everything from drug specifications to cell biology, cell proliferation, randomized, placebo-controlled phase, three study data and on and on and on. It took time, trial-and-error, and a lot of reading before I realized: People need more than that.

Yes, we need the facts and figures from John's talk. If you walk into a prospect's office and do nothing but appeal to them on an emotional level, they might like you, but you'll have zero professional credibility. On the other hand, if you go into that same office and do nothing but recite facts, totally ignoring the human factor, then you haven't established any human connection.

But the truth is—the "awesome" facts and figures that you recite to your customers don't make the sale because they don't create trust on a deeper level.

So, *what does?*

Sales needs an approach that aligns how we communicate with how the brain *actually* works.

An approach that establishes personal trust (selling to the limbic system and root brain) as well as professional credibility (selling to the neocortex).

But for at least two thousand years, Western culture has had it backward: We try to persuade people by starting with facts and figures. **We've been selling from the outside-in when we need to sell from the inside-out!**

After I finished eating, I pushed my plate back and said, "Let's think about it this way. What if Christina had gone first, connected emotionally to all of us like she did, talking about how you can make a bigger difference through how you're uniquely wired to solve problems for your customers. *Then* John got up and said, 'Here's how we can solve those problems for our customers, here's the gap, here's who you need to talk to, and here's what to say to them.'"

I let them paint that picture in their mind, then I said, "Same graphs, same tables, same information. How do you think it would have changed how you experienced John's talk?"

"Man! It'd be the difference between night and day!" a woman at the table said. "After Christina was finished, I was ready to go out and conquer the world!"

Exactly.

By the time you're finished reading this book, I want you to understand that the traditional sales training you've had teaches you to engage with only one part of the brain. Unfortunately for you, that so happens to be the hardest, most resistant, most skeptical, and least willing to change part of the human mind. To sell more and more easily, you need to engage with the other two parts responsible for emotion, empathy, visualization, trust, and connection. You also need to learn to sell in the right order: from the inside-out.

To understand the human brain, let's go back to how it all began.

THE CAVE-TO-CAVE SALESMAN

"People will teach you how to sell to them if you'll pay attention to the messages they send you."

—Jim Cathcart, Relationship Selling

IN MANY WAYS, one of the simplest ways to understand the buying brain is to watch the movie *The Croods*.

It's a story about a caveman family, led by the father, Grug Crood. He protects his family by adhering to a long list of rules, the most important of which was this: Anything new is bad.

New animal? Bad.

New person? Bad

New idea? Very bad.

Of course, there's a cataclysmic event and the family is forced to flee everything they've known and embrace change as a way of life. In the end, Caveman Crood realizes that change doesn't always have to be frightening. That status quo can be limiting to the very goals you have in life and that embracing change can not only be more effective, but it also can even be fun.

It's been a few thousand years since we lived in caves, but our brains haven't quite caught up yet. Millions of years ago, our higher level "thinking" brain, our neocortex may not have been as finely tuned as it is today. After all, there were far fewer websites to peruse or new iPhones to master. However, our emotional and instructive brains, our limbic system and root brain areas were essentially the same as they are today. Those parts of our brain keep us alive. Not only do they control breathing, blinking, and other involuntary things our bodies need, but they also control our instinctive and emotional reactions.

Nobel-prize winner Daniel Kahneman in *Thinking, Fast and Slow* as well as Malcolm Gladwell in *Blink* do a fantastic job of showing how much of our thinking happens in the subconscious—including judgment decisions. For instance, have you ever had a gut feeling about someone? You couldn't put your finger on it, but something felt...off? On the other hand, have you ever felt an instant connection with someone? Played a hunch? Fallen in love?

Those aren't rational decisions. If pressed, you could probably come up with some reason or excuse why you felt the way you did. But that approach ("Here's a decision—now, let me figure out how to justify it.") runs contrary to how we're "supposed" to think.

School teaches us to gather information in order to make an informed decision. We're supposed to "reason it out." Western thought and philosophy rests on this idea, reflected in the famous quote "I think, therefore I am." This line of reasoning by René Descartes harkens back to the Greek philosopher Aristotle. These two men and those who followed them saw the mind and body as two distinct entities. Consciousness (or rational thought) existed on one level; our bodily needs and functions existed on a lower plane of existence.

Until just a few years ago, many people, including notable researchers, thought that humans used logic to make rational decisions. Sometimes we might lose our temper or become infatuated and make an emotional decision, but once we were clear-headed, we'd return back to our baseline: reason. With this view, the way we've traditionally been taught to engage in sales and marketing makes sense. We present facts and figures, using logic and reason to convince a customer that our product is the superior choice. In other words, we appeal to their conscious mind.

The West has been wrong for over two thousand years. It's only been in the last few decades that we've come to understand just how inextricably linked our minds and bodies are. What scientists and researchers now understand is that what we think of as consciousness happens primarily in just one part of the brain.

But most of the activity in our brains actually takes place in what we know as the subconscious.

We don't make rational decisions, free from emotion and instinct.

Especially in a sales setting, we'd like to think that we're pretty smart, like a modern René Descartes. The truth is we're more like our caveman brother, Grug Crood.

How Your Customer's Brain Filters Your Message

In the 1960s, neuroscientist Dr. Paul MacLean came up with a concept called the triune brain theory. At the time, many other neuroscientists thought he was out of his mind (no pun intended). But what he proposed was that the **brain is essentially made up of three distinct layers.** And each of those layers is critically important on how we process information and make decisions.

In the ensuing years, medical science has discovered that the human brain is far more complex. But his model still stands as perhaps the easiest way for the layperson to understand the anatomy of the human mind.

The Outer Layer—the funky, folded, gray layer that we sometimes see on TV and popular movies—that's *the neocortex*.

It's basically the CPU of your brain. It's where you process all data, facts, figures, and features. *It's where you evaluate opinions and make rational judgments.* This part of your brain is an extremely efficient processor, capable of processing vast amounts of information.

The challenge with the neocortex is that it also tends to be the skeptical and judgmental part of the brain. As it receives that information, it judges it immediately. Data is either verified and validated or invalidated and dismissed.

The Second Layer—When we go down one layer from the neocortex, we see the *limbic system/brain*.

If the neocortex is your "thinking brain"—or perhaps another nickname for sales would be the "skeptical brain"—*the limbic system is your "feeling brain"*.

Areas like the hippocampus, the amygdala, the cingulate gyrus are areas in the limbic system *critical to* how we associate emotion with information and experiences in order to determine what we're going to do about it relative to our likes and dislikes, goals and objectives, opinions, and beliefs.

This is the area Hazel activated with her "peanuts = loaded gun" analogy. She triggered an emotional response to information the educators already had. But with a new emotion associated with it, their brain processed the exact same information differently!

One could argue that everything that's ever happened to you since you were in the womb gets encoded on little "neuron microchips" and stored in your limbic system. That information helps you or hinders you in how you perceive what's happening in your world today. So, believe it or not, things that happened to you all the way back when you were three or four years old got encoded—stuffed into what I call the "junk in your brain trunk." As you perceive information in the world around you today, information even that far back can and does guide your day-to-day emotional reactions and decision-making process.

The Third Layer—When you go down a layer deeper still, you've got the *root brain,* which we call the "instinctive brain": the cerebellum, brain stem, and other faculties in your mind where all your unconscious behaviors spring from. Things like breathing, hunger, avoidance, thirst, survival—all of those mechanisms and responses are being delivered through your root brain mechanism. Some researchers refer to this as the "R-complex" or "reptilian" brain.

> Here's how we filter information—from the inside-out, not outside-in. Our instincts and emotions drive decision-making. But we look to validate and rationalize those feelings/decisions nearly instantaneously with the facts and the data through the neocortex.[1]

Say I just gave you a big equation: I want you to take 757×625 and divide the answer by 3. Well, sure you could do it. To do so, your neocortex would be firing on all cylinders, essentially shutting off your limbic system and root brain because you're doing a mathematical equation.

Now, if I told you a factual data point such as, "At Braintrust, our clients see 150 percent increase in sales year over year. We have a 97 percent customer retention..." In that moment, your neocortex processes that information, and since it's data/facts, it's deciding rather quickly whether it believes it or not. If you know, like, and trust me, your brain will use those numbers as support for your belief (cognitive bias that we'll get into later) but if you don't know, like, or trust me yet, your brain will likely use those very same numbers as a reason to distrust or potentially disbelieve me.

It takes a lot more horsepower or energy in your brain to start with the neocortex and have it process this vast amount of facts, data, and information. If I get you emotionally engaged and tell you why I started Braintrust, and then tie it to why that matters to you followed by a compelling narrative around your challenges, something changes.

When you are following that type of an emotionally connected narrative, you suspend judgment of the facts.

It's important for us to understand as professional communicators how the message we deliver is being received and *perceived* by the brain of our audience.

If you're the type of salesperson who communicates primarily with facts, data, and figures, you're pummeling your customer's neocortex.

To recap:

- ✅ neocortex = your "thinking brain" (facts and data...skepticism, judgment, evaluation)

- ✅ limbic = your "feeling brain" (emotion, memory, internal visualization)

- ✅ root = your "instinctive brain" (safety, hunger/thirst, avoidance, survival)

When you go into a sales conversation, you need to think of these in reverse order: **Engage with the instinctive brain, then work up to the feeling brain, then—and only then—pitch to the skeptical brain.**

Information processing begins in their root brain. And it begins with the most basic question of: *friend or foe?* Then the root brain passes its determination along to limbic brain, which makes a determination: *fight or flight?* Not until it clears those gatekeepers and gets the greenlight does the information make its way to the neocortex for validation or further review.

> *You have to win over their instinctive and feeling brains first.* Until you do, you don't have permission to pitch to their rational, reasonable neocortex.

How do you do that?

Start by understanding our "self-preservation orientation."

Self-Preservation Orientation

Have you ever accidentally run into a good friend at the store or one of your favorite customers at the airport? You know when you recognize them and you automatically get a smile on your face because you're genuinely happy to see them? You smile because you feel happy; you're happy because your brain is flooding you with positive trust chemicals and your brain triggers those chemicals because it recognizes a friend.

Every moment of your day, your caveman brain is continuously scanning your surroundings, constantly asking: "Friend or foe? Friend or foe?" By nature, everyone is either "foe" or at best "neutral leaning toward foe" until our brain moves them into the "friend" category. In other words, potentially "unsafe" until I can determine you as "safe."

When you walk into a sales meeting, your customer's caveman brain already sees you as a potential threat.

The fact that you're there to sell them something only increases the threat level. You're the bad guy, there to get their money. You're already starting off at a disadvantage: As Captain Kirk used to command when the Starship Enterprise was in danger on *Star Trek,* "Shield's up, Mr. Sulu! Red alert!"

When the brain recognizes a potential threat, it triggers your adrenalin and spikes your stress levels, which is your brain's way of ensuring blood flows to your muscles to allow you to either stay and fight the threat or flee from it.

As the caveman brain goes into fight-or-flight mode, it redirects focus away from the reasoning neocortex to the fear-driven limbic system and root brain. Knowing that, doesn't it make sense why so many sales meetings feel tense or even confrontational? According to the caveman brain, it is! As humans, our instincts in these situations are to go into "self-preservation orientation." Shields up and phasers at the ready.

Now, "Captain Kirk" might listen to your sales spiel and hold off on firing phasers—he might even ask Mr. Spock about the logical course of action—but his shields are still up. Even if your customer is sitting in a Silicon Valley startup office that looks cooler than the *Enterprise,* his brain still *acts* like it's in the savanna, worrying whether a saber-toothed tiger is about to eat him.

But realize this: You do the same thing!

Your Neurochemistry in Sales Meetings

Sales meetings are stressful.

Even if you've been selling for so long that it doesn't really seem like stress, you can't fool your caveman brain. It knows exactly what this is. This is you hunting woolly mammoths, trying to survive another winter. The customer has money you need. It doesn't matter that we've gone from caves to houses and from spears to emails. Your caveman brain still automatically goes into flight-or-fight mode.

When the human brain is under stress—regardless of which side of the desk we're on—our neurochemistry changes. Our bodies are preparing us to either fight the threat or run away to live another day. Just like for your customer, your higher brain functions in the neocortex are impaired as the brain shifts focus to the limbic system and root brain.

Once we leave the sales meeting, we've all had those "Aww, man, why did I *say* that!?" moments. When our caveman brain perceives that the threat is gone and it can calm down, our higher-level thinking brain can switch back on. We can reason again and think through what we said and did during the conversation. But in the moment, we panic, and when we panic, we revert back to what we know.

One of my sayings is that **in a stressful situation, people revert to communicating from their highest level of ingrained training**. This is why the military trains our soldiers the way they do. In the heat of battle, soldiers can't rely on their neocortex. They have to rely on their ingrained training to see them through. On naval ships and submarines, they're constantly running practice drills. If a real fire breaks out on a boat, each sailor's fight-or-flight instincts kick in. The only way they can function flawlessly is by falling back on their instincts and muscle memory.

And what does the typical sales organization train or "ingrain" into their people?

Facts and data, features and benefits.

Whenever those same people go into a meeting that their income and livelihood depend on, their stress-hormone cortisol spikes, and they revert to their ingrained training.

No wonder things never change—self-preservation is a basic human instinct.

From a survival of the species standpoint, it's certainly the most important. When we experience pain or fear, we revert to our basic instincts: How can I survive this? What's safe? Our walls go up and our defense mechanisms kick in. Our instincts are to stick with what's safe and comfortable—what we know. Fortunately for us today, what we "know" may not get us killed like in the savannah, but unfortunately for many of us, it leads to the death of our sale nonetheless.

The False Security of Your Safety Box

On behalf of a medical device client, I once attended a medical conference with a group of surgeons in Denver. Over dinner, I had the chance to get inside their heads. I wanted a better understanding of where their mind was in those hallway conversations they have with sales reps between surgeries.

Specifically, given the data about how vastly superior my clients' tech was, why would surgeons continue conducting surgery the older, less effective way that put their patients at higher risk with less reliable outcomes?

After going back and forth with one rather exuberant, narcissistic surgeon, I decided to use some of my "voodoo" as one client so eloquently called NeuroSelling to tap into their limbic system. When he finally took a breath, I saw my opening and said, "Look, if I were your patient, I wouldn't let you put me on your operating table. You are choosing to ignore solid medical evidence in favor of older methods proven to be less effective and more harmful to me as a patient. I wouldn't be comfortable having you operate on me or someone I love."

My goal wasn't to make him mad. I purposely played devil's advocate because I knew that if I could spike his stress hormone, cortisol, I'd get an emotional response (instead of a rational, thought-out answer). Finally, one of the surgeons blurted out the heart of the matter: *They didn't fully understand the technology and they weren't comfortable using it.*

Put another way: "I pride myself on knowing exactly what I'm doing, having the answers, and being the expert, so I'm going to stick with what I know. This product is new. It's different. I don't want to be the guinea pig in my circle of peers. I don't want to try something new and wind up looking like a fool."

From their point of view, you have to appreciate where they're coming from. A stranger is standing in front of them, trying to sell them something, quoting medical studies in journals they may or may not have even heard of. They expect the salesperson to cherry-pick the "facts" that will land them the sale. They also know that for every medical study touting the prowess of their device, there may be a dozen that find contrary results. It's not that these medical professionals don't practice evidence-based medicine.

It's that they don't trust the word of yet another medical salesperson trying to sell them something.

> They're not going to buy *until they believe* their current way of practicing puts them or their patient at more risk than a new, different way; they're going to stay in their comfort zone (safety box) until they feel comfortable or forced to venture out of it. They're going to stay where it's safe until you prove to them something new is also safe *and* better.

Yes, even high-IQ, logical, rational people like doctors and surgeons still function like Grug Crood. **New is bad. New is risky.**

That's really the case I'm making in this book. Until your customers feel their current way of doing things (status quo) becomes riskier to their self-preservation than the new alternative you're proposing, they're going to stick with what they know...and so would you. There you are, a perfect stranger, telling them it's safe to venture away from what they know. Of course you're going to tell them that—that's how you make money.

"You don't know me from Adam, but here's something new and different, you should buy it, and by the way, I make my income from convincing you to do that—but trust me, that doesn't affect my recommendation!"

Our survival instincts tell us to stay where it's safe until we know it's safe to do otherwise or at minimum, less safe where we are.

Telling them about the features and benefits of your product doesn't persuade strangers because they've been conditioned to *not trust the source.*

No one takes the *National Enquirer* or *Weekly World News* seriously. They're tabloids spouting the latest Elvis sighting or the most recent Bat Boy capture. We know we can't trust the source, regardless of how many "experts" the tabloid article cites. (I'm not saying that surgeons necessarily put medical reps in the same category as supermarket tabloids but follow my analogy here.)

It doesn't matter what features your product has, how wonderful your service is, how superior your technology is, how many studies you cite, or what benefits you promise—you are a new person and they believe you're going to look out for #1 (because that's certainly what they're doing) therefore, you likely cannot be trusted. We trust people and sources who've proven to be trustworthy. By default, everyone outside of that circle of trust gets put in the box of "not trusted."

So how do you get into the circle of trust?

THE NEUROSCIENCE OF TRUST

I ADMIT IT: I'd procrastinated.

When I boarded the plane, I was days behind on some of the administrative tasks that are my least favorite part of being CEO. Thankfully, I'd been upgraded, so I'd have plenty of room to work. I already had my laptop out and started booting up when a mother, father, and son boarded the plane. The mother and son began settling down in the row ahead of me. It looked like the father was going to be sitting beside me.

Now, I'm a sociable guy, but I had a lot of work to do and was really looking forward to knocking it out in this two-hour flight. I stared hard at my screen as I began feverishly typing, hoping I looked too busy to bother. Well, the dreaded fifteen or twenty minutes from the time the boarding door closes until that glorious "ding" that tells us we are above ten thousand feet was the window my new seatmate used to "get to know me." I couldn't even use the "headphones in, even though they aren't connected to anything" trick as I had left them in my bag in the overhead bin.

The moment we began pushing back from the gate, he immediately started chitchatting. I said to myself, *Well, I guess this is how it's going to be.* So, I turned toward him in my seat, gave him a warm smile, and picked up the conversation. I've learned that my real purpose in life is being available for these very conversations. I never know why, but usually there is a divine reason meant for either me to learn something from someone else or to add value to that person in some meaningful way, so my initial frustration with not getting work done quickly gave way to my past experiences in human connection.

When he asked me what kind of work I did, I started with the same story I tell everyone: "Well, what I do really has to do with *why* I do it. I'm an old farm boy. I grew up on a hundred-acre farm that my papaw bought..."

After I'd shared my story, I invited him to tell me about himself. He started talking about his life and we spent the rest of the flight swapping stories and ideas.

When we began our descent into Denver, he asked, "So what does Braintrust actually *do?*"

I said, "We teach people how to communicate with their customers in a more impactful way—from a place of "why" versus "what" based on the science of human behavior."

"Oh?" he responded. "What's that look like?"

"Well, you, for example: I understand where you're coming from. I understand your 'why.' You grew up on a thousand-acre cattle ranch in Colorado, learning life and business lessons from your father and grandfather. They taught you about honesty and integrity, like the time that you watched your grandpa have a chance to keep an extra hundred dollars at the stockyards if he'd have just kept his mouth shut—but he didn't. He spoke up, pointed out the old man's mistake, and paid him the extra hundred dollars. When you started your wealth management firm twelve years ago, you wanted to do business the way you saw your grandpa do business. And that's why it's important to you today that you do the right thing, even when you think nobody's watching."

My airplane buddy sat there, amazed. "Holy cow! How did you get all that from my story?"

I replied, "I told you my 'Why Story.' You instinctively opened up and told me yours."

He said, "You know, I've never told anybody many of the details I shared with you in my story. Not even my wife," he said, gesturing to the seat in front of him.

"Why not?" I asked.

"You know? I don't know, but that's a great point."

On Sunday morning the next weekend, I woke up to see a text from him: "Can't thank you enough for that plane ride. Last night I shared my why story at our company party. Not a dry eye in the house. Changed the whole feel. THANK YOU."

Now, when he asked what I did for a living, why didn't I tell him about Braintrust? Why not give him the standard "Oh, I'm a [insert job title here]"? Why did I answer his question by telling him about my "why"? Why did I *not* tell him how I made my money until the second time he asked?

Because he didn't really care what I did. He was just making polite conversation. Small talk that you expect from your seat buddy.

It wasn't until I'd opened up about myself and shared a deeply personal story—that is to say, something that made me vulnerable—that he felt a real connection to me as a person. Then, without prompting, he shared something deeply personal to him. Something, in fact, that he'd never even shared with his own wife of many years sitting right in front of him!

Once he saw me, not as a stranger, but as a relatable person, he wanted to genuinely know what I did.

This time, instead of asking out of expected politeness, he asked out of genuine interest. When we were landing, he volunteered to exchange phone numbers so we could keep in touch. That's the power of a Why Story.

Even though he was clearly someone we could help and I was the person with something to potentially sell the minute I realized that, he was the one asking if we could continue the conversation.

The Science of Connection

Grug Crood doesn't open up to strangers.

The idea of being vulnerable with someone not "friend" is foreign to him.

And vice versa.

When I displayed vulnerability—when I shared something that was intimately important to me—my newfound airplane friend's caveman brain said, "Oh! A story. Let's listen." His mirror neurons activated. Then once he realized the depth of story I was sharing, his caveman brain went, "Oh! Vulnerability. Then this guy isn't a foe—foes don't share personal details like this. Therefore, he must be a friend." His "trust chemical" oxytocin surged.

It's not manipulation. It's learning how to connect and communicate with other human beings in a day and age when our caveman brains are more hindrance than help.

That's why Christina relating her intimately personal experience in the leadership development program created such a profound moment and connection.

By being vulnerable—and let me emphasize, *purposefully* vulnerable—you speak directly to the limbic and root brains. Popular researcher and author Brené Brown says it like this in her book, *Daring Greatly*:

> *Vulnerability is the birthplace of love, belonging, joy, courage, empathy, and creativity. It is the source of hope, empathy,*

accountability, and authenticity. If we want greater clarity in our purpose or deeper and more meaningful spiritual lives, vulnerability is the path.[1]

The most important thing is to speak from the heart. You can't be vulnerable and cagey at the same time. Your listener can tell if you're being insincere or inauthentic. *To create real connection, you have to be fully authentic and be willing to show it.*

You know why Christina is so passionate about that leadership course. You can see for yourself that I'm carrying on Papaw's legacy of storytelling from my personal "why" story you read earlier.

So, when I say to you, "That's why I do what I do, tell me why you do what you do," I rarely get the other person's resume. They don't say, "My company works with—" They recognize that the mood has changed. I just shared an authentic story with just the right amount of vulnerability about how I grew up, and why, thanks to my Papaw I believe what I believe through what he taught me. That sets the tone for what I'm expecting out of them.

Your Why connects more people to what you do than your What and How. The Why is your passion and reason...share it and see how people reciprocate and connect...every time.

In Part II: The Field, we will introduce you to a road map of stories that, if built the right way and delivered in the right order, will drive trust faster and create an urgency for the prospect to change. The first story you will learn to create is your personal "why" story. The moment that prospect or customer believes that you're believable, there's a connection and that connection leads to trust.

You may believe that you couldn't possibly create a Why Story. I've heard hundreds of people say those very words. But everybody has a story. And I mean everybody. Everybody comes from somewhere. Everybody has a reason for why they do what they do. We just have to help you find yours and then teach you how to communicate it the right way at the right time, just like Matt Rogers...

The Power of the Personal Narrative

Early in the first day of a two-day NeuroSelling workshop, I could tell Matt was the ringleader of the salespeople in the group. He was built like a defensive lineman and, as I learned, he had, in fact, been a football player in college. He also had a gregarious personality and natural charisma about him (which helped when he'd been on *American Idol*—the guy was just all-around impressive).

But in the two-day workshop, I could see he was struggling with the part of the training where we help people write their "Why Story." What's a Why Story, you ask? Well, think back to chapter one where I told you my Papaw story, then ended with why teaching neuroscience and narrative-based selling is personally close to my heart. I embedded why I do what I do inside of a memorable story.

Of course, it's not easy. But when you get it right, *man,* is it effective!

Seeing that Matt was having some challenge with the exercise, during a break, I pulled him out into the hall and said, "What's up, big guy? What's got you stumped?"

He said, "I don't know what to write about. I just don't have a motivating story."

I said, "Well, tell me a little about how you grew up."

"I didn't have a great childhood. My dad wasn't really around so I was basically raised by a single mom."

"Okay," I prodded, "tell me about her."

"My mom? Gosh, she's amazing. I don't know how she did it. She worked two jobs to keep me and my brother in clothes. And our clothes didn't come cheap because we were both big guys."

He went on for a few minutes, then I asked, "So what do you feel like your mom taught you? Any examples you can remember?"

"Yeah: she taught me a lot about sacrifice, serving others and thinking about others more than yourself. Even though we ourselves were poor, every Saturday morning we had to go down to the homeless shelter and serve food to others my mom considered far worse off than us. That was her thing. I'll never forget one time—I was probably thirteen years old—and I wore a size fourteen shoe already. I had been saving up my money from doing chores and odd jobs so that I could finally have a pair of the new Nikes. My mom had been saving up as well as she wanted to match what I saved to help me out. I had my eyes on these shoes for months and months. After a lot of hard work and saving, I finally got that pair of Nikes I wanted. I was so happy. I'd never had anything nice like that before. We didn't have money, so this was a big deal.

"Well, that Saturday, we went to serve at the homeless shelter. I remember it was a really chilly morning. On the way in, we walked past a homeless guy sitting on the side of the street. My momma stopped to talk to him like she did with everybody and invited him inside to get a hot meal. Then she looked down at his shoes. They were too small, so he'd cut the toes out so he could wear them. His toes were just sticking out and I remember thinking how cold that must have felt."

Matt stopped here, choking back tears as he recounted the rest of his story.

"She told me, 'Matt, take off your shoes and give them to this man.' I was bigger than my momma, but she was one of those women you just don't argue with. So I gave him my shoes, and then she made me put on his. Otherwise, I'd have gone barefoot.

"I was devastated. I'm watching this guy walk around the shelter, get his food tray, all while wearing the Nikes I've been saving up to buy for nearly a *year*. When we got ready to leave, I thought she was going to make him give them back, but she didn't. We just got in the car and drove home, me with my big, size-fourteen feet sticking out of these ratty, stinking shoes, with my toes now freezing.

"And then she said this to me: 'Matt, I don't want you to ever forget this: You will never know what someone's life is like until you walk in their shoes.' And as sad and disappointed as I was in that moment, you can bet I've never forgotten that."

By the end of his story, he was choked up, I was choked up, other people were passing us in the hall wondering what was going on, but I said, "Matt, why would you say you don't have a Why Story? Get your butt in that room and start writing!"

He went on to craft a personal Why Story so engaging the entire workshop gave him a standing ovation after he told it at the end of the class. And here's the thing, he volunteered to do so. As I often quote Mark Twain, "The two most important days in your life are the day you were born and the day you discover why." Matt certainly did just that.

Six months later, he called me from his cell phone.

"Jeff, I've got some good news. At the workshop, I was number 183 out of 300 salespeople in our company."

Not sure where this was going, I said, "Okay?"

"Well, you know the story I didn't have, that I really did have?"

Of course, I remembered. Who could forget a story like that!?

"Well, next week, I'm getting recognized onstage as the top salesperson in my division and one of the top in the entire company! And it's all because of my Why Story."

I said, "Alright! Man, that's awesome!"

Matt said, "When I go on a sales call, I barely make it past my story when they say, 'I don't even care what you're selling, I'm buying!' It's been unbelievable."

Take a wild guess at what Matt sold. What came to mind? Life-saving pharmaceuticals? Life-changing coaching? Paradigm-shifting consulting? World-changing technology? Would you have guessed outsourced payroll and HR?

What is it about Matt's narrative that took him from the bottom half of his sales organization to the top? He starts each sales conversation, not with facts and figures aimed at the logical neocortex, but by first connecting on a subconscious level. He establishes *personal* trust.

All this goes back to how our brain processes information and makes decisions. We make decisions that make us feel safe. We feel safe with information we trust. We trust information that comes from trustworthy people. We trust people we connect with.

Ditch Rapport. Build Trust.

When I say personal connection, most sales professionals hear "rapport building."

Repeat after me: *Rapport building does not mean you've established personal trust.*

In fact, you've probably never been taught how to build a personal connection in a business environment. Think about it: How much time in your career have you spent in classes, trainings, workshops, reading, and learning how to build genuine personal connections in a business environment? Most of the sales techniques you've probably heard are around "rapport building," a quick-and-easy, superficial, artificial, transactional, self-serving gimmick to trick people into trusting you. (Even if your intentions were pure, your motive is still self-serving.)

The one I tend to see over and over again looks a little something like this: You walk into a sales meeting, look around, and see the customer has a picture of themselves on a sailboat.

"Why, Mr. Smith, I see you have a picture of a sailboat on your wall. You like sailing? What a coincidence—I drink water! Looks like we already have something in common!"

That sounds amateurish when you read it in black and white, but I cannot count the number of professional salespeople selling multimillion-dollar products who do this type of rapport building attempt, maybe not word for word, but believe it or not, this is likely how it comes across to your customer. Maybe it's a picture of their spouse, children, pet, or hobby. Regardless, the salesperson tries to find some way to identify with the customer: "Oh, you have kids? Me, too! Man, aren't they great? Okay, let's talk about your software needs!" Does it feel like that approach creates a personal connection? Or does it sound like an impersonal attempt to get their business? The hard thing for us to accept is that the customer knows exactly what you are doing. They've seen that movie a thousand times before with a thousand other salespeople. Here's the thing: no matter how genuine you come across using this type of technique, you can only create, at best, a superficial level of trust. Not the type of trust that drops the shields.

As soon as their caveman Grug Crood brain sees you as a transactional "can I get you in a new car today?!" type, it thinks, *Okay, here's another salesperson trying to get our money. Enemy alert—shields up!* Their cortisol spikes. Instantly, their brain goes into defense mode and begins filtering everything through the lens of risk and skepticism.

You know what doesn't spike?

Oxytocin.

The Trust Chemical

Oxytocin is a neurochemical/neuropeptide our brain produces after a mother gives birth[2]; binding the mother and child together[3] as well as fathers[4]. Researchers have nicknamed it "the bonding hormone," "the love hormone," or sometimes "the cuddle hormone."

The oxytocin in our brain rises when we interact with our "in-group": individuals we've identified as friend, not foe.

We feel it when we play with children, even if they're not our own. While oxytocin is closely related to mother-baby bonding and breastfeeding, foster and adoptive parents still create high oxytocin levels.[5] *Oxytocin solidifies our connection with others and is why we feel protective of them.*

We would do things for our in-group that we would never consider doing for strangers.

We experience a rise in oxytocin when we interact with our pets.[6]

Oxytocin also reduces our feelings of fear and anxiety,[7] actually counterbalancing the effects of adrenaline and cortisol triggered by our brain's fight-or-flight instincts. We've discussed how our customer's defenses are already triggered by a sales meeting. Encouraging oxytocin can help moderate those instincts.[8] Perhaps even more importantly, **higher levels of oxytocin mean higher levels of perceived trustworthiness.**[9] At high enough levels, research suggests that it can overcome breaches of trust. That is, even if you do something to me, if I have enough oxytocin, I'll still trust you despite your actions.[10]

Simply put, oxytocin determines how much I trust you, hence, we call it the "trust" chemical. Dr. Paul Zak is a neuroeconomist, researcher, teacher, and author of *Trust Factor: The Science of Creating High-Performance Companies* and *The Moral Molecule: How Trust Works.* What he found was that when two human beings interact and there is the perception of care, connection, empathy and trust, oxytocin levels are high in both participants.[11]

Harvard Business School professor Amy Cuddy has been studying first impressions for more than fifteen years and has discovered patterns in these interactions.

In her book *Presence,* Cuddy says that people quickly answer two questions when they first meet you:

- ✅ Can I trust this person?
- ✅ Can I respect this person?[12]

Interestingly, Cuddy says that most people, especially in a professional context, mistakenly believe that competence (credibility) is the more important factor. After all, they want to prove that they are smart and talented enough to handle your business, right?

But, in fact, what she found was that **personal trustworthiness is the most important factor in how people evaluate you** and when they feel that way about you, oxytocin goes up in both parties!

Cortisol, a.k.a. "the stress hormone," is the antioxytocin.[13] When my caveman brain is in "friend-or-foe, fight-or-flight?!" mode, it overrides whatever oxytocin I had as my stress is triggered. And until my brain moves you from the category of foe to friend, my cortisol will remain high.

So how can you get my oxytocin flowin'?

With what I call the elements within the "Periodic Table of Trust."

PERSONAL TRUST ELEMENTS   PROFESSIONAL TRUST ELEMENTS

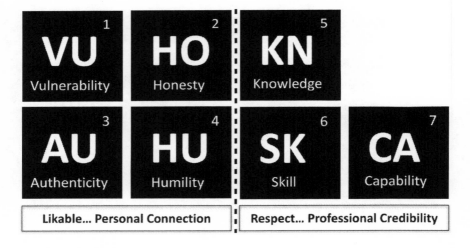

Remember: *Not until someone trusts you personally will they allow you to help them professionally.*

There are two types of trust. *Personal trust and professional trust.* Personal trust comes from connection whereas professional trust comes from credibility.

> You have to display the personal elements of trust to trigger their oxytocin. Then, you can demonstrate the professional elements of trust to make and validate the sale.

But as a sales professional, I'm probably not telling you anything radically new. Vulnerability and humility may be two pieces of the puzzle you're not quite sure are a good fit for how you sell, but it's not particularly groundbreaking that people buy from people they like and respect.

However, from my experience, there's a really good chance you may be doing it in the wrong order, leading with credibility while assuming you have a connection that isn't nearly as deep as you believe.

When it comes to the balance of personal trust (connection) and professional trust (credibility), I like to look at it through the lens of pop culture and movie characters. Do you remember the movie *Dumb and Dumber*? ("So, you're telling me there's a chance!") Would you buy anything from Lloyd Christmas? Of course not; he's a self-absorbed moron. No connection. No credibility.

Would you buy anything from Chris Farley's beloved *Tommy Boy?* We can't help but love him, so we might buy something from him out of kindness. But it'd never be anything of consequence. Good connection but lacking credibility.

What's the difference between Jim Carrey's character and Chris Farley's? Likability. One had zero emotional intelligence and the other was a wonderful connector. Neither could earn our professional respect. One could earn our personal trust, but that's only half the battle.

Tommy Boy's reluctant sidekick, Richard (David Spade's character) was his opposite image. He knew all the answers, but he was just a plain jerk. Nobody liked him. High professional credibility, low personal connection. You might buy from a salesperson like him if there's no other game in town, but you wouldn't go out of your way to do it. And you'd probably switch to someone else who was just as credible but more likable as soon as you got the chance.

Or you could buy from Matt, the *American Idol* football player: high, wonderful personal connection backed up with strong professional credibility. If we were to chart all four of these people on a table, it'd look like this:

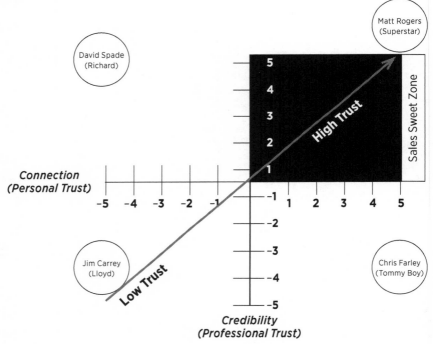

Let's examine what Matt has that these other three don't.

Think back to the periodic table of elements hanging on the wall in your high school chemistry class. Metals were on the left of the chart; gases were on the right. All were elements on the table, but some were grouped together because of the way they behaved. In NeuroSelling, I group the "elements" of trust into two types: personal connection and professional credibility.

Read the following two statements:

1. People buy from people they trust. They trust people they like. And they like people they connect with.

2. People buy from people they trust. They trust people they respect. And they respect people they find credible.

Both statements are true. Unfortunately, too many salespeople only know how to use pieces of each concept. They try to create some kind of rapport, hoping their customer will buy from them because they feel a personal connection (the Tommy Boy route). Or, they might open up the firehose of facts, features, and information, hoping to drown them into a sale with their product knowledge and credibility (the David Spade route). Neither approach is effective.

Traditional sales training revolves around helping us be perceived as more credible to the customer—not connectable. And again, knowing your stuff is important. If you've made a connection but not established your credibility, then you're Tommy Boy. But if all you do is attempt to establish credibility without establishing a connection, then you're David Spade...Richard.

Worse, if you use a gimmicky rapport-builder like the hundred other sales reps who've walked into the customer's office, then you're actually *hurting* your personal connection. You've signaled that you're a salesperson who doesn't really care about a personal connection and is just there for a business transaction. You're really looking like David Spade now. To be Matt, moving from the lower half of your sales organization to the top half and then *numero uno,* you need all the elements of trust—all seven of them.

How can you get started?

The Miracle of Mirror Neurons

You can't fake honesty.

Not in the long run. But it's hard to create a genuine personal connection in the short-run, especially in a fifteen-minute sales meeting. Or it was, up until we discovered **mirror neurons.**

Mirror neurons play a big role in empathy: feeling what someone else feels.

When we see something happening to another person, our brains automatically begin to replicate or "mirror" that person's experience.[14] Researchers first came across mirror neurons while studying monkeys' brains. One monkey happened to be eating ice cream. Another monkey was sitting across the room. The researchers saw the second monkey's brain start firing away as if it were eating ice cream too!

Come to find out, humans are wired for mirror neurons as well. When we watch *America's Funniest Home Videos* or bloopers on YouTube, we can sometimes feel their pain (guys, you exactly know what I'm talking about!) or their embarrassment. The brain recreates those scenes in our own minds via mirror neurons.

When a human being can demonstrate empathy to another human being, something magical happens.

Author and researcher Richard Boyatzis (who wrote *Primal Leadership* and *Helping People Change*) and his research partner Anthony Jack found that empathy is critical to relationships as it activates the portion of the brain related to emotion and relatability, but suppresses the area of the brain that's typically active in the activity of nonemotional analytical processing.[15]

> In other words, when you come across as honest, authentic, and humble with the right amount of vulnerability, you will likely activate the empathic network in your customer's brain. When that happens, it will deactivate all the "noise" of the judgmental, analytical portion of their brain.

When Christina was up on stage sharing her story of attempted suicide, she didn't know she was firing up our brain cells. But that's exactly what happened. Our mirror neurons heard her father telling "us" that we weren't good enough and experienced sadness that followed. We felt lonely with Christina while at college and experienced that heartbreak as her family broke up. We felt that searing desperation when she tried to take her life.

But then we felt a ray of hope as she went into recovery. We all had a little twinge of "aww" when she found someone who loved her for who she was. We felt elated when she discovered her purpose and found a way to walk in her truth. Christina took us on an unforgettable journey, an emotional rollercoaster—not to manipulate us, but to share her experience with us.

Later, while having lunch with some of the attendees, I asked them if they trusted Christina. Every single person responded "Absolutely!" There wasn't a person in that ballroom who didn't feel a personal connection with Christina...someone who'd been a perfect stranger to many of them just fifteen minutes earlier.

Our mirror neurons didn't fire during her introduction about the leadership course. She was delivering facts, figures, and data. It wasn't until she began relating her personal experience that she got our brains engaged.

Researchers named them mirror neurons because our brains begin experiencing the same things we see others doing, whether that be literally "seeing" or the picture our minds imaginatively paint. We experience empathy because our brains are attempting to internally replicate what's happening externally.

When we watch a movie on TV, our neocortex knows that, rationally, we're safe on the couch inside our own home. But as we watch the characters on screen, our mirror neurons begin firing—even with a fictitious story! Do you remember the raw emotion we felt at the end of *Avengers: Infinity War*? One of my friends sat there in the movie theater, too stunned to move. Think of that "aww" moment when Forrest Gump put his son on the school bus. We all felt triumph in *Remember the Titans*.

When you tell someone a story, the same movie effect happens. We don't need a movie screen in front of us because we have one in our head.

When our brain begins to fire the neurons related to our empathic network, our higher reasoning quiets down. Consciously, we know we're not experiencing what we're hearing. But unconsciously, our brain is replicating that experience in our mind. But instead of settling into fight-or-flight mode, we unconsciously move the narrator into the friend category. Our empathy induces oxytocin and we begin engaging in the story, same as the narrator. Our mirror neurons begin firing on the same wavelength as theirs.

> Researchers have brain scans showing that when a narrator begins speaking, listeners' brainwaves begin subtly adjusting to match the narrator's. Our mind identifies the narrator as part of our "in-group" of people just by virtue of the fact that we're in their story with them.

When you walk into a sales conversation with me, you want to make a personal connection. You want my cortisol to go down and my oxytocin to go up. The best way to do that is to get my mirror neurons firing. The best way to do that is to give me a narrative that my mind will automatically follow along *with* and relate *to*. My mirror neurons can't help but begin to fire as my mind recreates *your* story in *my* head!

Don't forget that this is not just great for the customer. It's incredibly helpful for you as well. As we tell a story, we're also producing oxytocin in our own brain. We feel ourselves bonding with the person we're speaking to with the very same chemicals parents have when bonding with their children. We're unconsciously going to go further and aim higher for this new addition to our in-group, just as we would with others. In other words, just by virtue of doing this exercise, we're creating a partnership with the person on the other side of the desk—a human-to-human connection, not just "rapport."

But it can't be just any narrative. Don't walk into my office and tell me the story of Cinderella. That's not going to accomplish our respective goals. **Your story needs to be one that displays the personal elements of trust: vulnerability, honesty, authenticity, and humility.**

You can't fake those.

That's really the beauty of NeuroSelling. The people who don't deserve to sell to customers—those who would lie and manipulate just to earn a quick buck—*can't be both authentic and inauthentic, or honest and dishonest at the same time.*

Which is precisely why Matt went from the bottom half of his company's salesforce to winning an award on stage for being at the top. Yes, he used the rest of the NeuroSelling methodology, but it was his Why Story that did most of the initial heavy lifting. As more than one of his customers told him, "I don't know what you're selling, but I'm buying!"

That's the power of personal connection backed up with professional credibility. Due to the "inside out" nature of how our brains operate, once I trust you personally (limbic and root brain), then my neocortex begins looking for reasons to support the rest of what you're telling me as truthful and useful to me and what I care about. Conversely, if I have doubts about you from a personal trust standpoint, my neocortex begins seeking out reasons to confirm that "feeling"; therefore, I start poking holes in your credibility and looking for reasons to reject you... even with the very same information that I may have otherwise accepted if I trusted you!

> If I were selling for your company and I had thirty minutes with a prospect, I'm going to spend the first fifteen to twenty minutes ensuring I have a genuine, personal connection and show the customer I actually care about what they care about before I ever introduce a "problem" that I believe I can help them solve. Unfortunately, many salespeople spend about five minutes or less "connecting" and not really even connecting before they roll into their "needs analysis" and nauseating product dump.

For those who may be thinking there has to be more to this than just an effective connecting "why" story, you are correct. That's just the beginning.

Now it's time to find out how you really feel about change. Not what you *think* about it, but how you *feel* about it...

5

THE PHYSIOLOGY OF CHANGE RESISTANCE

"Resistance to change is proportional to how much the future might be altered by any given act."
—Stephen King

I'D LIKE YOU to pause for a moment and think about the life you've created. From the job you have to the home you live in to the relationships you've developed—from your spouse or significant other to your closest friends. Now, just for illustration purposes, I'd like for you to imagine that in the span of just a few months, your house catches fire, your spouse asks for a divorce, and your boss tells you that your services are no longer needed. This scenario, as unimaginable as it may seem, was the unfortunate case for James. He certainly wasn't looking for this to happen, didn't *choose* for any of it to happen, yet like it or not, his life had dramatically and suddenly changed.

In our live workshops, I frequently ask the group, "By show of hands, how many of you like change?" Inevitably, about half the room will raise their hands.

Then I rephrase the question: "How many of you like change that was chosen for you or forced upon you, that you didn't initiate?" You start to see the hands slowly go down in the room. Nobody likes feeling forced to change.

What is it about change? Why are human beings resistant to it? Why do we especially resist change when it's not our idea, even when it's a rationally better option?

Now, in James's case, those certainly weren't better options but he certainly didn't choose for them to happen. As you might imagine, James feels that change is bad. In fact, most, if not all humans feel the same way.

For instance, I once worked with a client several years ago who decided that, instead of having laptops for their sales organization, they were going to roll out tablets for everyone—all two thousand sales-people. The strategy behind the change was sound. Better flexibility, more versatility, and the sales team would look more "tech savvy" to their customers.

Put yourself in the salesperson's shoes. Your status quo is your laptop. You understand it. You know how it works. You've been using it for years. It's been your number one weapon as you left the cave each day to kill something and drag it home.

Suddenly, your boss's boss's boss says, "We're taking away your laptop. You have to use an iPad now. It'll be great. Good luck."

If you were an early tech adopter and liked the latest gadget, you would probably already have a personal iPad, so you'd be excited about this change: It's change you welcome or even *wanted* because it aligns with how you see or feel about yourself! By definition, though, most people are not early adopters. Most people like to go with something that's proven, especially when it's how they make their living. The vast majority of those two thousand people were unhappy, frustrated, or even angry.

There is a very big difference between the change that *we choose* versus change that we feel like someone else forces us to do.

If you come to me with something that challenges my current status quo, it feels like you're challenging me personally.

You're confronting my beliefs about myself, work, and my previous decision-making.

You're telling me, "Jeff, what you've been doing all this time is wrong. My way is better. You need to change."

In fact, that was almost literally my message to those surgeons at the conference I previously mentioned. Of course, it triggered them, that was my goal. They had to explain to me in a moment of emotion, the reason behind their change resistance.

When you challenge someone's status quo either intentionally or unintentionally, the other person's inner Grug Crood speaks up: "Change is bad. Anything new is bad. New ideas are very bad." Their cortisol spikes and their stress mechanisms start firing because *their brain doesn't know if it's safe.*

The threat of change triggers our self-preservation orientation.

When you walk into a sales conversation, you're asking your potential customer to leave their comfort zone. You're telling them they need to change. Who likes to be told they're wrong? Who likes to be told they need to do something better?

No one. Ever.

Change is not fun. All of us already feel like we're overwhelmed as it is just keeping up with everything we're already doing. Then someone like you comes in and tells me I need to learn a new feature, try out a new service, take time out to experience a new widget? You're not *just* trying to get me to leave my comfort zone. You're not *just* trying to overcome my self-preservation orientation. You're pouring gasoline on all the fires in my life. I don't want gasoline—I'm trying to put the fires out!

When you approach your customers, it doesn't matter how much better things could be for them if they'd only buy what you're selling. As the great Dr. Henry Cloud once said, *"We change our behavior when the pain of staying the same becomes greater than the pain of change."*

That's such an important concept that it deserves its own block quote reworded to fit today's sales professional:

> Your customer won't change until they believe that what they are doing today is less effective and more painful than doing something different with you tomorrow.

When speaking with your customers—and especially when speaking to them for the first time—it's incumbent on you as a professional communicator to understand a few specifics around **barriers to change.** We will focus on what I believe to be the top six barriers. These are driven largely by the limbic brain (the feeling brain) and the root brain (the instinctive brain).

You need to be able to articulate a message that puts your customer's mind at ease so they're willing to go along with you on this change journey. As an aside, when it comes to implementing the concepts throughout this book, you will also potentially be challenged with doing something different with the way you communicate so naturally, that you will experience these barriers as well.

Barrier 1: The Anxiety Avalanche Effect

In Gary Keller's book *The ONE Thing,* the founder of the global realty company Keller-Williams talked about "the clench":

> *You might say that I started to clench my way to success. I really did. I thought that this might be the way you went through life—with your jaw clenched, your fist clenched, your stomach clenched, and your butt clenched.*[1]

Fortunately, he discovered a better way forward than simply living in a constant state of elevated cortisol, always in fight-or-flight mode. But it's a great visual to keep in mind when you are going into a customer conversation...for both of you.

Even if you're an experienced sales veteran pulling down seven figures, you can't fool yourself: Your brain knows that you're walking into an important, high-stress situation. Your body will be under stress. You may have far less stress than when you first began your career, but there's no way for you to completely switch it off. Each of these conversations could be the difference between hitting quota or not. Your self-preservation orientation automatically triggers—the clench.

You have to realize that the same "clench" reaction is true for your customer.

You may have more riding on the outcome of the conversation than they do, but regardless of the context, I guarantee they have heightened anxiety too. I might be used to a parade of salespeople coming through my office or operating room, but just the fact that you're not in my in-group *and* you're trying to get something from me immediately triggers my self-preservation orientation. My adrenaline kicks in, my anxiety rises, and cortisol is spiked, no matter how confident I am or may appear to be. My limbic and root brains know exactly what's going on. You're an unknown, you want me to leave my safety box and charge off into the wild unknown. Nope. Not happening.

> The reason for that anxiety is that your brain can't perfectly predict the outcome. In other words, **fear of the unknown.** The way our neurochemistry works, when we feel anxiety, we tend to isolate ourselves. Our self-preservation orientation kicks in and we retreat to our closest safety box, which for most customers is status quo and for most salespeople is rambling on with their highest level of training...your product details.

How do you overcome this barrier?

It's not by appealing to my logical mind. Mr. Spock might have been the Vulcan aboard *Enterprise,* but the irrational, fly-by-the-seat-of-his-pants, shoot-from-the-hip human being James T. Kirk was the captain. Presenting things like testimonials, social proof, lab results, clinical trials, and data-driven schematics isn't going to persuade Captain Kirk to lower his shields. Not until he trusts the source of that information. Mr. Spock is the captain's sounding board, but Jim's in charge of the ship.

To counteract the cortisol, you have to get the oxytocin flowin'. That means a narrative embedded with the elements of personal trust to get their mirror neurons firing.

Barrier 2: The Desolation of Isolation Effect

Recall those two thousand reps suddenly forced to switch from laptops to iPads. They got frustrated. Even angry. There was a mass outcry and pushback. Some business managers often chalk these types of reactions up to "people just hate change" and direct their employees to suck it up, in so many words. Fortunately, my clients weren't cut from that cloth, they listened in earnest to their sales reps. And you know what they discovered was the real problem?

The vast majority of those reps felt isolated.

Human beings don't do well with isolation. I'm not talking about being lonely or being locked up in solitary confinement. This barrier to change is about feeling like the Lone Ranger—in a bad way. Feeling like they're the only one out on the prairie, trying to fend off the outlaws and bad guys while getting little recognition and help in return.

With all two thousand being geographically dispersed, they didn't have an opportunity for watercooler talk. They didn't know that many of the other 1,999 reps felt the same way they did. They intuitively assumed everybody else was successfully making the transition, while they alone struggled with making the switch. Each one felt like they alone had been left out in the cold to fend for themselves.

When you walk into my office asking me to change, you're asking me to ride even farther into the Wild West. To use another cowboy metaphor, you want to cut me off from the herd. That's how lions and cheetahs catch their prey: by isolating the weak from the pack and killing them individually. I feel safer if I remain with my herd.

(Sure, some customers like being on the bleeding edge of technology and methods, but they're not going to make a major business decision just because they want to be one of the cool kids. Even with them, you need to remember that you're up against their potential feelings of isolation.)

In today's more complex B2B buying environments, there is usually more than one person involved in the buying process. You might think that this would spread the impact of a bad decision across more decision makers which, in turn, would decrease the feeling of isolation, but it tends to have an almost multiplication effect. *Each person in the process feels the pressure of being the lone person to recommend the change and the politics within organizations can cause prospects to fear being the only person on their team to advocate for the "risk of change."*

How do you work with this barrier to change?

Simple: Make sure I don't feel isolated. Create a personal connection with me so that I feel like I have a partner willing to go with me, not someone who's just there to make the sale and hand me off to technical support. *Show me that I won't be the Lone Ranger:*

Who else has made the switch?

What's been their experience?

Do you have any social proof to show me that others have walked this path before?

Have you been able to connect the various decision makers and influencers in my organization in a way that creates a more visible and "team" approach to our buying process?

Finally, have you been able to show me how not changing actually puts me and the goals and objectives of my role at risk?

If you switch my perspective and mind-set, that resetting can help remove my fear of isolation by helping my subconscious focus on our next change barrier...

Barrier 3: The Fear of Loss Effect

The psychology behind our fear of loss fascinates me. We've lived in a world of scarcity for so many generations of cavemen that it's etched into our collective human subconscious. Starving to death was more than a real fear: It was a reality. Finding a good source of food, water, or shelter was rare. When our ancestors did, they guarded it with their life because it often *was* a matter of life or death.

Even if that's not the reality for you or me anymore, our brains haven't caught up. We're hardwired to hold on to what we have and literally fear its loss, whatever "it" is. We've immortalized this in the age-old proverb "One in the hand is worth two in the bush."

When you present me with the option to do something different, you're saying, "Jeff, I know you have done what works for you—even if it really doesn't—but here, try this. You'll love it. Trust me."

You're asking me to give up what I know in exchange for some unknown. I may not like where I am, but I'm afraid of losing what I already have. You're asking me to gamble my job or reputation on whatever you're selling.

Since my brain prioritizes not losing what I already have, and my natural inclination is to view change as bad or risky, therefore, I will lose. Use that as a frame when you engage in customer conversations.

> It doesn't matter how great your new product is: Your customer's mind is more worried about what they stand to lose than they are motivated by the promise of what's to come. In fact, as we'll cover in chapter six, the Nobel prize-winning researcher Daniel Kahneman discovered we are *twice* as motivated by a fear of loss than the prospect of gain. I hate to say it, but fear *is* the best motivator. The problem is, when you communicate the wrong information, in the wrong order, my fear of losing what I have will drive me deeper into change resistance.

But I'm not a fear monger and you shouldn't be, either. I've found a way to use this change barrier in a way that feels authentic, not sleazy.

I reframe the customer's problem by introducing a new point of reference: **What do they stand to lose if they *don't* act?**

In fact, you spike your customer's cortisol with this angle, not enough to kill their oxytocin, but enough to trigger a slight surge of adrenaline, helping them focus on their real problem (the one you're helping them with).

When their focus goes from the risk of trying something new to the certainty of doing nothing, this barrier to change flips into a motivator: They want to run away from loss as fast as possible!

Barrier 4: The Options Overload Effect

My wife owns and runs a creative meeting venue in Cincinnati called Brainstorm. (Yes, I had influence on the name and yes, I may be a little too obsessed with the brain) Nonetheless, she has two locations.

One downtown and one in the suburbs. Recently she called me in a bit of a panic. She had events going on in both locations on the same day. Believe it or not, both venue hosts called her at 6:00 a.m. and had forgotten their keys and couldn't get in. The caterer who was supposed to deliver breakfast to the downtown location showed up at the other location causing breakfast chaos to ensue.

On her way to the venue to let her employee in, my wife received a call from a neighbor downtown that a crane putting in new windows on the floor above hers accidentally knocked in the back wall of her venue with the crane. Then, just for fun, the fire marshal called her just a few minutes later to inform her of multiple changes she needed to make to the venue to avoid being out of compliance. This all transpired on the same morning, while I was out of town and Hazel was trying to get our seven-year-old daughter, Priya, ready for school.

Have you ever had a day like this or a season like this? Maybe even a year like this where it seems like "When it rains, it pours."

Well, like a good husband who believes "problem solvers rule the world," when my wife called to tell me this almost unbelievable cascade of events, naturally I went into problem-solver, superhero mode. I began to list off in rapid-fire fashion a solution to handle each situation. I could hear my wife's voice start to break on the other end. She had hit the breaking point. As humans, we can only take on so much before we start feeling overwhelmed. **We can only take so much change at one time and so many choices or options for solutions to that change before our brains just shut down.**

Your customers feel the same way.

When you start talking about all the things your products and services can do and all the possibilities you offer—and, indirectly, all the things that need to change—their mind goes into overload. It can feel like you're trying to change too many things at once. That triggers stress which triggers cortisol which triggers "shields up, Mr. Sulu!"

Simple, incremental change is much more impactful and easier to adopt than throwing everything at them, including the kitchen sink. As a sales professional, you probably know that rationally, but do you practice that? Do you intentionally try to simplify every customer conversation you have? Or do you unload all the features and benefits you can possibly sell them? If you'll remember our earlier discussion, under stress, you will communicate from your highest ingrained level of training. When you're operating from a stressful standpoint yourself, your innate desire will be to attempt to sound credible and to do so, you feel the urge to unload the vast wealth of facts and figures you have rattling around in that neocortex of yours. Overwhelm mode, indeed.

That's why the thrust of chapter eight is all about gaining a deep understanding of your customer's "hair on fire" problem, then solving that one problem with value clarity and only that one before moving on to the next. Yes, that runs counterintuitive to what you've probably been taught and practiced. If you have a live one on the line, you want to reel them in with as much as you can, right? But the more new information the human brain has to process, the more likely it will simply shut down, triggering the person's self-preservation orientation.

Remember: Choosing anything new = *risk*
Choosing multiple options of multiple solutions =
overwhelming risk

In a high-level sales meeting, you need to be strategic, intentional—surgical, almost—in where you lead the conversation.

Barrier 5: The Scarcity Syndrome Effect

Now, the fifth major barrier to change is that we tend to feel like *we don't have enough resources to implement the needed change.* This is a common one, especially for sales and marketing leaders who feel like they have unrealistic expectations placed upon them and their teams that they simply can't meet. You might feel the same way yourself, like you don't have enough prospects or that you don't have enough tools and systems.

Now, I'm just going to be real with you: I've found that this is usually an excuse. It's a conscious explanation of a subconscious feeling. Implementing this change or achieving a big goal feels overwhelming. Grug Crood does not take risks. Grug Crood lives in a world of scarcity, fighting for his life every day. Grug Crood lives in a world where he barely survives.

I already have problems with bandwidth. I'm already afraid of losing what I'm risking. I already worry about walking this path alone. Unless you can convince me that I have everything I need to succeed, my default is to assume failure.

The more you talk to me about the million-and-one things your gizmo can do, the more work I hear. My hair's on fire as it is—I don't have time to do all the stuff you're asking!

> This barrier is typically wrapped around a perception of lack of time, money, resources, or knowledge. *If that's my worry, what's your solution?* I need the picture of what's going to happen when I inevitably run into trouble.

What kind of support do you offer? Am I going to be on my own (linked to the fear of being isolated from the herd)? What are the contingency plans? Better yet, supply the narrative by telling me about a customer who ran into a challenge and how it was handled.

My caveman brain already perceives a reality of scarcity.

Calm my nerves and prove me wrong. Show me that you have all the resources I could ever need to help create a smooth change process or implementation.

Barrier 6: The Safety Box Effect

The sixth and last barrier we're going to talk about is probably my favorite barrier of all.

When the pressure to change is off, what happens?

We revert back into our safety box.

You see, we've built safety boxes everywhere in our lives. As long as we're in one of our safety boxes, guess how we feel? You guessed it: safe! The minute someone asks us to step out of our safety box, all of these barriers to change instantly pop up.

We don't want to change. And if we can somehow get rid of the pressure to change, we get to go right back to where we feel comfortable: the status quo. And in a sales conversation, guess where they feel the pressure is coming from? So, if they can get rid of you, they get to go back to the realm of status quo!

You see this concept play out every January 1. Everyone's excited about their New Year's resolution. This is going to be the year we finally lose weight and get fit. Thousands of people join the gym. You can't find a free machine and everybody's using all the equipment. But you know human nature. You know that if you're patient enough that by the end of February the gym will be empty again and you can go back to your normal routine.

Why?

The pressure to change is off. New Year's is over. The resolution's over. "Meh...I'm not really *that* out of shape."

The same thing happens in our customer conversations.

If we don't give our customers a compelling enough reason to change once we leave, guess what they do?

Head right back to their safety box.

Remember: *People don't change until the pain of staying the same is greater than the pain of change.*

You've experienced this dozens of times without realizing it. Your customer will be excited at the prospect of working together, you shake hands, and walk out. The next time you talk to them, you can immediately tell that something's happened. Their excitement has cooled. You hear the worry in their voice. They start going back over issues and potential problems that you thought you'd put to rest.

It's not their fault—it's just human nature. In his book *Misbehaving: The Making of Behavioral Economics,* behavioral economist Richard Thaler wrote, "In physics, an object in a state of rest stays that way, unless something happens. People act the same way: they stick with what they have unless there is some good reason to switch." Inertia pulls us right back into our norms. And our norms are fear, scarcity, isolation, and the desire to be warm and comfortable back in our comfy, albeit somewhat cramped, little safety box.

Where I used to be perplexed, these days I recognize that I'm simply dealing with basic neuroscience. I go back to basics and make sure I've addressed the most important questions:

- ✓ Have I gained their personal trust and professional respect?

- ✓ Have I identified the problem most important to them?

- ✓ Have I framed their problem in a way that demonstrates what it's going to cost them if they do nothing?

- ✓ Have I shown them an easy way to avoid that loss?

- ✓ Have I framed my solution as the best way to solve their problem—not as facts and figures, features and potential benefits, but as the only logical choice to solve the very problem that's preventing them from accomplishing their goals?

✓ Have I proven that others like them have had success doing the same thing?

✓ Have I proven that they won't be alone as we implement my solution?

When it comes to change, it's critical to remember that your customers and prospects don't like it any more than you do. In fact, by you telling them they need to change, you are not only triggering all the aforementioned physiological change resistors, but you are also doing worse. You're telling them that they are poor decision makers and what they've chosen to this point is wrong. Understanding what's happening at the subconscious, physiological level can really help you frame your conversation in a much more productive way. In the end, your prospect has to feel they are *choosing* to change.

So how do we do that? First, we must understand the psychology of belief and the very biases that may either propel us toward change or drive us farther away.

THE PSYCHOLOGY OF BIAS

"A man generally has two reasons for doing a thing. One that sounds good, and a real one."

—J.P. MORGAN

THIS CHAPTER IS another foundation-laying chapter. If you'll stick with me, I promise the payoff is worth it in Part II: The Field, when we start bringing all of this together for your next sales conversation.

Depending on what research you look at, there are somewhere between fifty-three and one-hundred-and-four cognitive biases.

"Cognitive bias" is a blanket term that refers to the ways in which the context and framing of information influences our judgment and decision-making.

There are many kinds of cognitive biases that influence individuals differently, but their common characteristic is that—in step with human individuality—they lead to judgment and decision-making that potentially *deviates from rational objectivity.*

In some cases, cognitive biases make our thinking and decision-making faster and more efficient. The reason is that we do not *stop to consider all available information, as our* brain, as the highest calorie-consumptive organ in the body, is looking for efficiency through shortcuts. In other cases, however, cognitive biases can lead to errors for exactly the same reason.

I could spend all day talking about the psychology of buying, but when you narrow it down to the cognitive biases most meaningful to influential conversations, I believe there are **six biases** that you really need to have a working knowledge of.

These six biases are driven by the interplay between the limbic system and root brain (the feeling and instinctive brain areas) and the neocortex (the thinking, rational brain). They are:

1. Prospect Theory (Loss Aversion)

2. The Anchoring Effect

3. Confirmation Bias

4. Availability Heuristic

5. Choice-Supportive Bias

6. The Bandwagon Effect

Cognitive Bias 1: Prospect Theory and Why We Hate to Lose

Here's a bizarre but telling game.

You have $0 right now. I come up to you and give you one of two choices: I will either give you $50, no questions asked and you walk away... or we can flip a coin: Heads you get $100, tails you get nothing.

Which would you pick?

Again, you have nothing right now. You have absolutely nothing to lose. Sure, you could take the $50, but for really good odds you could get double that! You have a one-in-two shot of winning the jackpot. When presented with choices like these, people overwhelmingly choose the safe bet of taking the $50 and walking away. Why is that? Why settle for less when there's a 50 percent chance of getting double at *zero* cost to you?

The answer lies in a book you may have heard of, *Thinking Fast and Slow*. The author, Daniel Kahneman, won a Nobel Prize for his research showcased within it. His research is chock-full of surprising insight. For instance, he found that human beings have two systems of thought or decision-making, the aptly named System 1 and System 2. (Obviously, his PhD was not in marketing.)

System 1 is our gut, instinctive feelings. We see a person and size them up in a split-second. I'm not saying that's a good thing, but it is how our brains work.

System 2 is our more deliberate thought processes. It's us thinking through the order of ingredients we need at the supermarket or working out a math equation in our head.

In NeuroSelling language, System 1 would be a combination of the root and limbic brains and System 2, the neocortex.

But while researching how we make decisions, Kahneman discovered something every salesperson needs to know.

The **Prospect Theory: Basically, it says that people don't make decisions based on the final outcome but based on the perception of potential gains and losses.** In developing the theory, he stumbled across something sales and marketing people have known—or, at least suspected—for years.

People are twice as motivated to change/take action or remain tied to inaction by potential loss as they are potential gain. It's why you and I would almost certainly take the $50 and walk away happy rather than flipping the coin for a one-in-two chance of $100. You see, our brain has already taken ownership of the $50, so anything that would put that at risk drives our decision-making. The fact that we really had nothing to begin with is a distant memory. Now you're asking me to "risk" $50 for the hope of more. I fear losing my $50 far more than "potentially" gaining $100. My brain becomes fixated on the horrible outcome of being back to zero. This is not logical. It's 100 percent emotional.

> When you present a solution to your customers, you'll find more success activating their fear or "risk" of loss versus talking about how much they stand to gain. You can give me a message that tells me all the things I stand to gain, or you can subtly weave a narrative around what I potentially stand to lose with my current status quo. My brain will only assign so much "value" to the benefits or advantages you're touting. *However, when you tell me what I stand to lose if I don't change, my brain assigns twice the value to what you're saying.* It applies twice the urgency to make a decision.

So, this idea of avoiding a loss versus pursuing a gain in our sales and marketing message is really, really important. Now, it's not about fearmongering.

You're not trying to go out there and scare your customers to death.

It's about **crafting a narrative** that really **highlights the problem** and the **risk associated with not solving the problem,** versus how great and wonderful your product is.

All your competition is likely out there with a gain, gain, gain message. (Unless they've already gone through NeuroSelling, in which case you're in big trouble.) "Here's our product, here's how great it is, here's why we're the best, here's why our customers say you should buy our product." That message—and, by association, everyone who says it—becomes white noise. My brain tunes it out.

But when I hear what I'm potentially about to lose, it grabs my attention. The reason?

Because problems evoke emotion. Products evoke judgment. Remember: *decisions are made inside out...emotionally first, then justified with facts and data.*

Talking about what I stand to potentially lose will be processed in my limbic as a "problem." By our very nature, we know unsolved problems can put us at further risk and that is what the brain wants to avoid at all costs.

> Did you know that, according to **Sales Benchmark Index,** nearly 50 percent of forecasted deals end in "no decision" with nearly 60 percent of all sales not lost to competition but rather the dreaded "status quo."[1] That's almost two out of every three. Your biggest competitor isn't the competition—it's indecision!

That's why, in order **to drive urgency** to change, you have to frame the problem, *not* as the cost of acting, but as **the cost of inaction or taking the wrong action.**

What do they stand to lose if they do nothing?

Again, I'm not talking about scare tactics. NeuroSelling is not about manipulation. Once you properly quantify the cost of indecision, you won't need to exaggerate or use hyperbole. The numbers themselves should create the urgency. Your job is to make sure they're looking at the right numbers.

Cognitive Bias 2: The Anchoring Effect

At its lowest point, the Mariana Trench is 10,971 meters.

Sounds deep. Can you picture how deep that is? Likely not.

Without any solid point of reference, it's hard for our mind to wrap itself around just how big of a number that is. Even converting it to standard measurements (for us Americans) and learning that it equals 35,994 feet doesn't help much. We need a point of comparison.

Would it help to be reminded that the average, low-end cruising altitude for an airliner is 31,000 feet? Think about looking out your plane window at how far away the ground is. The bottom of the Mariana Trench is 5,000 feet below *that*. Put another way: if Mount Everest were put in the trench, its peak would still be a mile underwater. Once we have a point of reference, then we can begin to grasp the size and scope of what we're dealing with. We refer to these points of reference as "anchor points."

> The interesting thing about the Anchoring Effect is this: When our mind has no knowledge for comparison, it will reach for the most recent point of reference from our own experience, regardless of what it was.

Our same loss-aversion researcher, Kahneman, and a colleague once conducted a study where they asked people to estimate what percentage of African countries were part of the United Nations. But first, the study participants spun a wheel of fortune. The wheel numbers went from zero to one hundred. One group's wheel was rigged to stop at ten; the other's at sixty-five.

Once the participants had spun and gotten their number (ten or sixty-five), the researchers would then ask the participants two questions:

1. Do you believe that the percentage of African countries which are part of the United Nations is higher or lower than the number on the wheel?

2. What do you estimate the actual percentage to be?

The people whose wheel stopped at ten estimated that, on average, 25 percent of African nations were part of the United Nations. The people whose wheel stopped at sixty-five estimated 45 percent.

What did the wheel have to do with international politics and participation in a global body? Nothing.

So why did spinning a random wheel cause one group to nearly double its estimate?

Because of the Anchoring Effect. It works even when there is absolutely zero relationship between two things.

The retail industry has been using this for years. "Was $299.99, Now $49.99!" *Oh, man, I'm saving $250!* Was the item really worth $300 originally? Is it even worth $50 now? Who knows!? It doesn't matter. It feels like a great deal because of our brain's point of reference or anchor point.

Retail salespeople use this tactic all the time. You present the customer with a price and let them experience sticker shock. Then you add in the discounts and *voila!* a new, better price. Instead of the price looking expensive, it looks like a bargain—I mean, just look at how much it was originally!

As a B2B salesperson, you're not selling cars and furniture, but you're still dealing with basic human psychology. When you're presenting your solution, what's your customer going to compare it to? What's their point of reference?

If you don't give them an anchor, their brain will select it for themselves. Their anchor point might be your competitor they met with yesterday. It could be the article they pulled up on Google five minutes before you walked in. It could be the wheel of fortune app they were playing on their phone.

Why leave it to chance? Why not give them a proper anchor point?

Again, nearly 60 percent of B2B sales meetings lead to no action.

Doesn't it seem reasonable that a proper anchor point could be the cost of the status quo? What's it going to cost them to continue doing nothing? What happens if they don't solve the problem they have?

Let me give you an example of how we set the right "anchor" with a sales executive looking to improve their sales effectiveness:

"John, how many salespeople do you have?"

"One hundred."

"What's their individual quota?"

"Roughly two million bucks each."

"What's your goal increase for the year?"

"Jeff," the CEO said, "come hell or high water, we've got to increase top-line revenue by 10 percent this year."

"Well, if I'm not mistaken, 10 percent of $2 million is $200,000, right?"

The CEO says, "Yeah...?"

"So, what you're really telling me is that you have a $200,000 per sales rep problem that has to be solved, correct?"

He frowned for a second, then says, "Well, yeah, I guess we do."

Here, I used the anchor effect.

If I've done my job correctly, his new anchor should have him thinking "what would I pay per sales rep to solve a $200K problem?" Instead of letting him silently create his own anchor points, I instead helped him anchor the eventual solution I will offer him with how they should have been measuring it in the first place:

What's the cost of not doing anything about this at all or the cost of doing something that won't work?

At $200,000 a rep, anything reasonably south of that begins to look like a bargain!

Now, take a step back and think of it like this: $200,000 increase per rep × 100 reps = $20,000,000.

That's the larger problem that's at risk. Is it safe to assume you could keep doing what you're doing and get halfway there? Probably, but that still leaves you $10,000,000 short! What would you invest to bridge that gap? One percent? Five percent? Ten percent? Likely all of the above if you felt confident it would get you the results.

This is simply spiking their cortisol...on purpose.

They see what they stand to lose by doing nothing, so they can avoid their fear of loss by going with your solution. I'll show you how to use this strategy later in Part II: The Field.

Cognitive Bias 3: Choice-Supportive Bias

Choice-supportive bias—also called postpurchase rationalization—is the **mind's way of confirming that a decision you made was the right one.**[2]

In fact, our mind *misremembers* the actual memory to convince ourselves that we made the right choice.[3]

This is partially what I came up against speaking to those surgeons at the conference in Denver. They'd originally made the choice to use the other surgical method. It didn't matter to them the original reasons (it was the best at the time) were no longer valid. Their unconscious choice-supportive bias prevented them—or, at least, hindered them—from objectively examining new alternatives.

In studying choice-supportive bias, one study found that company board members who voted for hiring the CEO were more likely to overlook their faults and stick with them through challenging times than board members who weren't.[4]

That is, just the fact they made a choice and were "invested" in a CEO automatically made them give the CEO extra slack—slack they wouldn't give if they'd become board members the day after the vote. In other words, at the subconscious level, if the CEO failed, so did they.

Studies have shown that voters who weren't certain about which politician to vote for before going into the polling booth showed increased confidence coming out. Just by the very fact that they'd made *a* choice increased their confidence that they'd made the *right* choice.

With your customers, be hyperaware of their choice-supportive biases. Whatever choices they've made in the past make sense to them (even if their brain has to make up some of those reasons since then). It doesn't matter that the whole reason they made the decision in the first place doesn't exist anymore. They'll create new reasons to justify their past choices. In other words, their brains say, "You made this choice. Therefore, it *must* be the right choice."

That's why starting with facts and figures, features, and benefits (selling from the outside-in) doesn't work. The mind can justify why a person's original choice was superior, even if that means rewriting the memory. **You're not selling based on facts but on feelings—especially the ones your customer is unaware of.**

> The great news is, if you can lead your prospect down the path of an effective NeuroSelling conversation that ends with them feeling as if they are "choosing" your solution to solve their problem, it will take a move of the Almighty to prevent them from going through with the decision. This is when the bias is actually helpful to you, instead of a hindrance.

The key is, I can't feel that you're telling me the choices I've made to this point were wrong.

I have to arrive at that conclusion and the conclusion to choose you all on my own. Once I do, I'm yours forever. Or until you don't live up to your promise. Which I'm sure will never happen.

Cognitive Bias 4: Confirmation Bias

Whatever your political stance, you almost certainly see news articles and online posts that confirm things you already know to be true. All the time. The danger is that **our minds give extra weight to the things we already believe and easily dismiss or explain away evidence to the contrary.**

If I believe Chevys are the best pickup truck on the market, I'm always going to find magazine articles and hear people's stories about how great they are. If I see a news story about a navigation error resulting in a wreck, I'll chalk it up to a fluke or a bad batch.

The human mind will go to incredible lengths to cling to its beliefs, using the neocortex to rationalize completely irrational behavior.

> Confirmation bias: We seek out and find only the information that proves to ourselves that we're right. It's thematically similar to choice-supportive bias. However, the difference is internal validation versus external. Our brains say, "Look! Here's an outside source that proves our idea—we *must* be right!"

In *The Psychology of Influence,* psychologist Robert Cialdini recounts the story of the cult who believed space aliens were coming back for them at midnight on a certain date. Midnight came and went. Scotty didn't beam anybody up. Some of the cult members came to their senses and realized they were in crazy town, so they left. But most of them stayed. Around 4 a.m., one of their leaders begins receiving messages that the aliens had changed their mind because the cult members had done such a good job getting everyone ready. Instead of facing the reality that someone was either scamming them or was outright delusional, the cult members renewed their zealotry and became even more engaged with the cult. In the absence of reason, their minds *invented* reason.

Let's bring it back down to earth for a moment. (See what I did there?)

> If your customer has a bias against your product, your company, or the way you comb your hair, do you know what won't convince them to change their mind? Pounding away at their beliefs with facts and reason. Their neocortex is a rationalization machine, able to deflect and dismiss anything and everything you say. **The key to overcoming bias is through emotion.**

There are a thousand heartwarming stories about people overcoming racial biases and ethnic stereotypes. Just about every time, it started with two people finding common ground, then finding connection, then finding friendship.

This is why your Why Story is so important to a successful conversation.

By finding common ground, sharing some universal beliefs, and then creating a connection, you've bypassed the potential confirmation biases the neocortex had at the ready. You've made "backdoor friends" with the heartwarming emotional brain.

Cognitive Bias 5: Availability Heuristic

I've learned the hard way that when I think about something, the first thing that comes to mind is usually incorrect. I have mostly life and my wife to thank for this.

My natural tendency is to fall prey to my availability-heuristic bias. Basically, my brain assigns more importance, weight, and validity to information I can easily recall or have immediate access to than it does to external information—and especially if that information contradicts what I believe I know. The result is that, unless I'm careful, I'll let my fears and beliefs override good sense.

You've probably met someone who doesn't "believe" in seat belts or that smoking can kill them. They'll say things like "I know a guy who lived through a car crash. They say if he'd been wearing his seat belt, he'd be dead. That's why I never wear the things!" "My grandfather smoked three packs a day all his life and lived to be ninety. You can't believe everything you read." They've extrapolated a dangerous set of beliefs from a very limited amount of information.

How does this apply to sales?

Say you were a tech vendor selling enterprise software. As part of your standard lead-in, you refer to how fast your business is growing in the industry and why the customer should invest in your cutting-edge SaaS.

That morning on the drive into work, however, your customer heard that the tech-heavy NASDAQ had its biggest fall of the year yesterday.

It doesn't matter that it ended higher than at any point in the first quarter. It doesn't matter that the overall trend of the NASDAQ is positive. The customer's availability heuristic gives more weight to what they can immediately recall.

Arguing with them by presenting facts and economic trends isn't going to change their mind. In fact, they'll probably just become more entrenched in their stance that things look bad for tech—they'd be better off just sitting tight until they see which way the wind's blowing.

> But once they buy into you on an emotional level, the availability heuristic begins to work for you. Their new connection with you becomes the new "overriding" information their subconscious uses to dispel the simple statement about the industry they heard on the way in to work. Once they believe in you, they will use that trust to drive "truth" over some random radio announcer.

Cognitive Bias 6: The Bandwagon Effect

Of the cognitive biases we've discussed, this is probably the easiest and most familiar. As human beings, we're wired to be part of the tribe. **We don't like going it alone or trying something first.** (Recall the change barrier of feeling isolated.)

Remember the old saying in the eighties "Nobody ever got fired for choosing IBM?" Big Blue had that kind of a reputation in enterprise-level business. Everybody knew about IBM. Everybody.

Have you ever stopped to wonder how much money IBM made just from people feeling that way? IBM was seen as the safe choice. Sure, there were a few other games in town, but when people are under pressure, they chose safety. In this case, safety in numbers, a.k.a. "the bandwagon effect."

In sales, I've seen reps spend so much time talking about options and potential benefits, yet they never use one of the most powerful cognitive biases—giving the customer a chance to get on the bandwagon! As we discussed earlier, there's safety in numbers. There's less risk when we move as a group than in being the Lone Ranger.

> The bandwagon effect allows folks to see that there's social credibility out there. There's a backup, there's people saying that choosing you was a win for them and they want to be associated with that. *Create a narrative and a message that allows your customers to realize that they're not the guinea pig* in this decision to choose your product. Lots of people have chosen it and here's what they've experienced.

We're wired to need that social proof and validation.

Your customer needs to know that they're not hopping up on this bandwagon alone. They need to know that others have tried this and found it safe. The more people who do something—our minds reason—the less dangerous it is. The safer they feel, the lower their cortisol. The lower their cortisol, the more they can engage with what you're saying and the more they see others are on board, the more FOMO or "fear of missing out" starts to work on your behalf.

Back in chapter five, we covered the brain's barriers to change. Here in chapter six, we've covered biases and how to neutralize them or even get them to work for you. But the best tool you have at your "change" disposal is actually your customer's amazing, storytelling brain.

Let's talk about the surprising neuroscience of narratives.

THE NEUROSCIENCE OF NARRATIVE

*"Never tell a story without a point and try
not to make a point without a story."*

—Papaw Willie Bloomfield

TOWARD THE BEGINNING of our workshops, I always share my Papaw story.

I know the old truism is true: *"People don't care how much you know until they know how much you care."*

Unless the people listening to me trust me as a person, I know their shields are going to stay up. Their neocortex is going to critically judge everything that comes out of my mouth. Sharing my Why Story helps them see me as a relatable human being, not just another talking head.

At some point later in the first day, I'll give them a rapid-fire pop quiz. (Do the exercise yourself: Pause for a second after each question and see if you remember the answers too!)

"How many acres was Papaw Bloomfield's farm?"

"A hundred acres!" everybody shouts out.

I don't even give them a moment to pause before the next question: "How long was his driveway?"

"Fifty yards!"

"How much education did he have?"

"Eighth grade!"

"What kind of tractor did he have?"

"John Deere!

"What was the color and make of his pickup truck?"

"Green Chevy Silverado!"

I'll stop and let them catch their breath, then I'll ask, "Now how in the world did you remember all that information, collectively, in unison?"

I love the slightly confused or even surprised look on their faces as they ask themselves the same question: *How DID I remember all that!?*

If they closed their eyes, they probably couldn't tell you what color shirt I'd been wearing all morning, yet they can recall details from a second-hand account told hours and, sometimes, days before.

It's not some kind of mass hypnosis or voodoo. I just know how to use neuroscience.

Narratives, Internal Visualization, and Recall

There have been lots of studies on information retention and recall. The way you communicate information will determine how it's received and ultimately stored in the customer's brain. How does that work? What I'm about to share probably won't surprise you since you now have a rough idea of how the brain is wired.

Studies by the *World Bank* and others show pretty consistently that 5 to 10 percent is about all you're going to retain of facts, data, and such information.[1] *The London Business School* as well as *Stanford University* did similar, fascinating studies on retention, though, teaching different groups of students the same information but in different ways.[2]

The first group just received the facts and data. The second group was presented the same facts and the data, but they threw in a couple of visuals. With the last group, they communicated the same exact information, but through storytelling.

The group that got just the facts and data retained about 5 to 10 percent. Not surprising. The group that also had a few visuals retained about 20 to 25 percent of the information. The group that received the information via storytelling retained between 65 and 70 percent—about triple!

Remember: *Narratives engage our limbic and root brain.*

We have an internal visualization mechanism that recreates the experience as if it were our own.

How does this internal visualization mechanism work?

I want you to read until the end of this paragraph, then close your eyes for a moment to "see" this in your mind's eye. Pretend you're standing on the street where you grew up. You're looking back at the house, the trailer, the condo, the apartment, or whatever you grew up in.

Can you see it? Do you remember it? Was it brick? Was it wood? Was there siding? Was the door red? Was it black? Was there an oak tree in the front yard? What did it look like?

You can start to feel your senses come alive. Could you hear another car driving by? Did you feel the wind blow? Do you remember any special smells from your neighborhood?

Right now, you're looking at the words of this book. That image travels down your optic nerve and gets reflected back on the occipital lobe of your neocortex. That's how you literally see with your eyes. When you internally visualize something, those recalled images travel via the hypothalamus region of the limbic system and get projected onto your imagination.

When I can get you to *see* something using your limbic system, you become completely engaged.

That information gets stored differently than facts in your neocortex. "Experienced" memories—whether real or not—get stored in long-term limbic memory.

Princeton University did a study where they showed that when the communicator uses a story-based or a visual storytelling approach to communicating not only does the brain of the listener light up in the right spot, but it also actually lights up in the exact same spot that the communicator's brain is lighting up as they're telling the story—just like the monkey watching the other monkey eat ice cream.[3]

This synchronization and harmonization of two brains when you're communicating through storytelling is exactly how the brain is wired to receive that information, assigning emotion to that information to help drive decision-making.

So far, we've been talking about internal visualization: relying on my mind's eye to create an image of the picture you're painting with words. But what if you took it a step further?

What if, instead of having them conjure up the images, you created the visuals?

I want to challenge you to think a little differently about the visual aids you may be using. Most sales and marketing professionals try to use facts and data as their visual aids (à la PowerPoint). As a sales professional think about your sales deck right now. How many slides is it? How many bullet points are on each slide?

Just know this: a bullet point is typically interpreted in the customer's mind as a nonemotional, lifeless data point. If that's how you're communicating, even on slides, you're communicating to the neocortex.

> Instead, use pictures, images, and visuals that tell a story—that are metaphorical or analogous in nature. They'll go much further in simplifying your message and making your message connect emotionally with the customer. *Stories can go where facts alone cannot.*

A B2B Narrative Example

As you can imagine, I've had plenty of business professionals hesitant to use narratives. It's basic neuroscience: I'm telling them that they should try something new. It's different than what they've been doing. It's outside of their safety box.

Of course, your inner caveman Grug Crood is going to say no.

They'll say that their customers are sophisticated or that they don't respond to cute little stories. They might say that they don't need or want to dumb down their information. But what they're really saying is "I'm not comfortable with this."

They don't realize that they're not only working against basic neuroscience, but they're also doing a disservice to their customers. Our brains can only process a finite amount of information in our short-term memory. Remember back in school when the teacher was presenting a brand-new idea? After listening to her lecture for an hour, your brain would feel overloaded. Your eyes would glaze over and drool would start coming out of the corner of your mouth. She might as well not even have bothered with the last ten minutes—you had mentally checked out waaayyy before that.

Our brains have higher recall when new memories are created in connection with existing neural connections. Here's an example: Let's say you're selling a brand new, state-of-the-art piece of software that does everything I could ever want in my business. From accounting to payroll to project management and CRM, it's an all-in-one solution.

You could start our conversation by telling me all the stuff it can do. I'll feel like I'm standing in front of a fire hydrant, but at least you'll have done your job, right? I tuned out three minutes into your spiel, but sure, tell me everything you possibly know about your product.

What if, instead, you took out your iPhone and said,

> *"Jeff, I remember when phones just made calls and sent text messages. I used to carry around a calculator, a laptop, and a digital camera. Shoot, I remember sitting in McDonald's parking lots with a Rand McNally map trying to figure out where I'd made a wrong turn and worrying that I'd be late for my next sales meeting. I thought getting a turn-by-turn Garmin was pretty high-tech.*
>
> *I can't imagine going back to those days. I have an app or three for each of those functions. My phone has a better camera than the digital one I used to carry around and I don't need to constantly take out the SD card and import my pics into my computer. I use my iPhone to do everything. In fact, more than I ever thought possible with just a phone. And with everything in the cloud, I don't have to worry about losing my phone or it getting stolen. I just pick up a new phone, log into the cloud, and I'm right where I left off."*

In my head, I'm silently agreeing. That's been my experience too. I remember when gas stations used to sell maps right by the checkout and how frustrating it was when I went to take a picture only to see **MEMORY CARD IS FULL** flash across the screen.

> *"Now, Jeff, that's how our SaaS platform works. You don't need one system for accounting and another for CRM, then outsource your payroll to a third-party. Nor do you need to worry about having a dedicated IT guy taking care of the server in your closet.*

Just like your iPhone, you have all the apps to run your business in one place and you don't ever have to worry about hardware. It's all in the cloud. Our product works just like an iPhone."

Instead of presenting me with new information, you activated information that I already believe to be true, then piggybacked on my existing knowledge to make a link with something else.

Grug Crood doesn't automatically smash it with a club because it looks like something that my brain has already accepted.

When your mind makes the connection with an experience or concept you already know, it forges a **neural link** between those two isolated stories. **Not only do you understand the other person better, but you'll also remember what they're saying better as well.**

If I go into a sales conversation and dump a load of random facts and figures, you're asking my brain to process and store all this stuff separately. The minute you make a connection between your new information and something I already know, my brain creates a whole load of neural connections. You'll literally engage more of my brain.

The Two Ways the Brain Stores Information

Quick question: how many outside doors did the house you grew up in have?

Did you immediately and automatically see your house in your mind's eye? Even if just for a few seconds, did a picture reel play in your head as you quickly went through and around the house counting the outside doors?

Those are memories your brain has stored visually.

Next question: could you explain mirror neurons to me?

Your mind probably didn't reach for a picture—you probably started thinking back to the words you read a few pages ago. We store abstract concepts like that verbally.

Not all memories are created equal.

You see, the brain stores memories basically two ways: verbally and visually.

Our visual recall is far stronger than our verbal recall.

It's why we can't remember the words to the Bill of Rights we learned in our high school civics class and yet know exactly what clothes we were wearing that time we seriously embarrassed ourselves in that same classroom. When you store information both visually *and* verbally, however, you have exponentially higher recall.

That's why facts embedded in stories are so much more powerful than facts alone. Jerome Bruner, the godfather of clinical psychology, found that when facts are embedded in narratives, people are *twenty-two times* more likely to recall them.

If, at the start of a workshop, I verbally listed those random facts from my story—a hundred acres, fifty-yard driveway, eighth-grade education, and a green Chevy pickup—almost no one would recall those details hours later. But because those facts were stored both visually (in their mind's eye as they "experienced" that story with me—ah, the power of mirror neurons!) as well as verbally, virtually everyone I try this with has near-perfect recall...on a second-hand story they heard from a total stranger.

Wouldn't it be great if your customers had near-perfect recall of everything you told them?

Now that you know the science behind how we store memories, achieving this is pretty straightforward: simply embed those facts, figures, and data in a narrative.

Let's go a little deeper into crafting effective narratives.

The Basic Elements of an Effective Narrative

There is a power in story, and it doesn't have to be the "once upon a time" variety. Great sales and marketing professional communicators understand that evoking a visual narrative is simply about using tried-and-true techniques to convey a message in different ways.

Some people are born storytellers. Papaw Bloomfield was one of them.

The great thing about NeuroSelling is that you don't have to be one of these people. You don't need to master the art of storytelling. Creating a compelling narrative isn't that hard because any story is better than no story. **You just need the basic elements and an elementary structure.**

The easiest and most traditional approach is the straightforward model we've used for centuries.

First, you need the setting. Then you need a **good guy** (main character/protagonist). The good guy has goals, hopes and dreams. Then along comes the **bad guy** (antagonist). The bad guy attempts to prevent the good guy from achieving his hopes and dreams. But alas, along comes **a sage**...a guide who shows the good guy a way forward. A way to overcome the bad guy. The good guy has to make a choice and take action. Then comes **the outcome** (did they succeed or fail?) and **the moral.**

From the tortoise and the hare to Cinderella to Odysseus: They all follow this basic structure. This structure follows the tried and true Joseph Campbell "hero" story structure.

Sometimes the bad guy isn't an enemy but a situation. For instance, picture two mice in a maze. Every day, they get up, race through the maze to find the big block of cheese, and then bring some back to their cage. One day, the smarter mouse notices the block of cheese has gotten smaller over time. He decides to start spending part of each day searching out the rest of the maze for a new block of cheese. The other mouse thinks it's a waste of time.

The smarter mouse finds some more cheese and starts memorizing the route to get there. Eventually, the original block of cheese is gone. The smarter mouse is fine because he's already been nibbling off the new block. The other mouse starves to death.

This simple business fable sold millions of copies of *Who Moved My Cheese?* and gave people an easy metaphor for a complex message: "We need to be innovating and finding new markets because one day our current market will be disrupted."

I've helped sales teams create hypothetical stories around everything from mountain climbing, preparing for tornadoes, and a floor supervisor in charge of a factory line. You don't need a riveting Shakespearian drama.

You just need a structured narrative.

In chapter nine, we're going to talk about the "5 Ps": the five narratives you need when walking into a sales conversation. Once you have this framework, you'll be able to create trust building, change inducing narratives for any given customer conversation. Now the fun begins. Let's take what we've learned in the lab and apply it in the field.

For Access to Free Bonus Tools to Help You Implement
the Concepts of NeuroSelling, go to:

www.braintrustgrowth.com/neurosellingtools

PART II

THE FIELD

START WITH WHO, LEAD WITH WHY

> *"Customer-centric…means you give the customers what they want rather than what you want to sell them."*
>
> —JACK MITCHELL, HUG YOUR CUSTOMERS

ONCE UPON A time, I coached individual executives, not sales teams.

It seemed that every time I sat down with a president or CEO, the conversation would go, "My biggest problem right now is we're not growing. If you can coach me through how to fix that problem, that would be huge."

In my head, I was thinking, *nearly every growth problem can be tied back to leadership…that's the whole reason we're doing this coaching! Let me help you!* But telling a CEO that his whole problem is between his ears isn't a particularly popular message.

Nor is it an effective way to help people. You see, because I understand how the brain works, I knew that the CEO's self-preservation orientation was triggered. His worry was "If I don't right this ship, the board's going to throw me *over*board. How do I save myself?!" Until we could solve that problem, his brain was hyperfocused on the imminent threat. As long as he felt like he was in the trenches under fire, there was no way I could pull him into the general's tent and talk long-term leadership development.

With these clients, I finally realized that, before I could earn the right to speak into their personal development, I needed to help each of them address the overwhelming problem in their professional life.

"Alright, sometimes it helps to have fresh eyes on the situation or just an objective third-party in the room. Let's get your VP of sales in here, maybe your head of marketing, and see if we can do something different."

That approach eventually morphed into the foundation of the three programs we teach at Braintrust, NeuroMessaging, NeuroSelling, and NeuroCoaching. But my point is this: My customer couldn't hear what I had to say over the deafening noise of their immediate fear/problem. **They couldn't focus on what really *needed* to be fixed until they were certain we corrected what *had* to be fixed. Sales.**

If this is true for the person sitting at the very top of a company, don't you think the same is likely true for all the rest of your customers?

Sales Doesn't Start with Why

Author and speaker Simon Sinek is spot on: Before anything else, you need to know your why. As he rightly states, "People don't buy what you do, they buy why you do it."

Having a Why Story is right up his alley. You need to understand what influences you before you influence others. But when it comes to communicating with people, you don't start with why.

You start with "who."

If John, our VP of sales character from our previous story had been an outside motivational speaker instead of the VP of sales addressing a ballroom full of his employees, he likely would have acted differently. His tone and content would have been tailored for that audience. He also would have acted differently if he'd been presenting to a roomful of customers or, still yet, in the conference room of a big potential customer.

All of us act differently, depending on the situation.
We communicate one way with our coworkers, another way with our long-time customers, and yet another in first-time sales meetings. Perhaps the better example would be Christina. Because she was speaking to her coworkers already inside the organization, she could go out on a limb and talk about her attempted suicide—probably something she wouldn't share with, say, a stranger on a plane. (And certainly not with the TSA agent during security.)

To create change, your focus has to be the other person. Christina didn't share her story because she wanted a group therapy session. She did it because she wanted everyone in the room to see how transformative the leadership program was.

Studies have shown that one of the most important traits of consistently successful salespeople is the ability to be empathetic—seeing the customer conversation from the other perspective. In the popular *Harvard Business Review* article "What Makes a Good Salesman?", the authors concluded from their research that it boiled down to just two traits: empathy and ambition. They wrote:

> *...the salesman with good empathy...senses the reactions of the customer and is able to adjust to these reactions. He is not simply bound by a prepared sales track, but he functions in terms of the real interaction between himself and the customer. Sensing what the customer is feeling, he is able to change pace, double back on his track, and make whatever creative modifications might be necessary to home in on the target and close the sale.*[1]

Empathy in the moment is good. But you don't need to be a great reader of body language and other nonverbal clues to be empathetic. You can "prime" yourself to be empathetic by doing your homework *before* you're in front of your customer. That's the kind of functional empathy you need to be able to cultivate.

NeuroSelling isn't about gimmicks and in-the-moment tactics. It's about a systematic communication approach with your customers as you continually understand them, their roles, and their problems at a deeper and deeper level.

Understand your customer. Start with who.

Problem Solvers Rule the World

Recently, on a plane ride to a speaking event, the TV in the seat back in front of me began to play that all too familiar "safety" video. "Hi, I'm Joe Blow, CEO of SuperAir"—real airline CEO name and brand omitted to protect the innocent—"We've just finished a multimillion-dollar rebrand of our entire fleet..."

I immediately tuned out. I don't care about a new paint job on the tail fin. Does not affect my life at all. I'm two weeks behind on email, presentations, staff development, personal development, and, oh! I haven't gotten my daughter Grace anything for her birthday yet.

This may come as a surprise, but **your customers don't really care about what you're selling.**

- ⊗ They don't care about how many bells and whistles your gadget has.

- ⊗ They don't care about how many awards your R&D team has won.

- ⊗ Let's bring it closer to home. They don't care about your quota.

- ⊗ They don't care about helping you make commission.

- ⊗ They don't care that your job may be on the line.

- ⊗ They don't care about making you look good in front of your boss.

They don't care about your problems at all.
What do they care about?
Their own problems, of course.

Yes, that's right, self-preservation orientation strikes again.

What would they welcome more?

Someone there to solve the problem that has them losing sleep.

They're worried that their job performance may not be up to snuff. They're worried that someone else is after their job. Or they may be worried about something at home. Their relationship could be on the rocks. They might be having a tough time with their kid. Their parent might be in the hospital.

When you walk into a customer conversation, you have to stop thinking about your problems. "Can I get this person to buy?" "Can I get a meeting with their boss?" "Is this going to be my big sale this quarter?"

Instead, take a page out of Matt's book and walk in their shoes. What's their hair-on-fire problem and how can you solve it?

And you can't simply call what you sell a "solution."

It doesn't matter what label you slap on the box: It's not a solution unless it solves their problem.

Your problem is that you need to sell something. That's not their problem. That's yours.

When you sit down with someone, you need to know what their self-preservation orientation is. What's threatening them? What are they most concerned about telling their boss they haven't solved yet in their next one on one meeting?

Frequently, I like to ask salespeople this question, **"What's the Number One job of a salesperson?"**

They answer, "To sell more!" "Make quota!" "Get more customers!"

Wrong. That's what's important to you, the salesperson and your boss. Those answers are all *results* of doing the only thing that creates those answers- **solving your customer's problems.** (Remember Papaw's truism: "Problem-solvers rule the world.)

Subconsciously, we all need to start with "who." We tailor our message and presentation to whoever's sitting in the other chair. But you need to be explicit about it. I want you to start doing it intentionally.

> When you're in your next meeting with a customer or prospect, try to see how long you can go without talking about your product or your features and benefits. I know it can feel counterintuitive, but your focus can't be on selling your stuff. You're there to solve their problem *with* your stuff. The salesperson who can hold off talking about their solution the longest usually wins.

The Impact of Inverted Insomnia

Let me give you an example you're probably familiar with and one I'm intimately familiar with. When I walk into a sales meeting, I know what I need our customers to buy: our NeuroSelling program. My business supplies the salaries for me and my staff. Our families depend on our incomes. I need to provide for the people who depend on me, personally and professionally. I need to cover the cost of our properties and upkeep.

But the person on the other side of the table isn't losing sleep over my issues. I am. They're not worried about how they can help me make payroll. Far from it.

What are they losing sleep over? That's the focus. Unfortunately, we tend to invert the focus of the sleepless night to our own insomnia. Ironically, when your primary focus is helping your customer stop losing sleep by solving their critical issues, the resulting impact is, you also tend to sleep easier.

In our world, our primary customer is a CEO, VP of sales, or chief sales officer. What's their worry? What triggers their self-preservation orientation? After working with so many of these folks for so long, I can tell you their top three or four typical objectives:

1. Increase top-line revenue

2. Decrease sales cycle time

3. Decrease the amount of discounting to get new business

4. Decrease sales rep ramp-up time from hired to producing

If they accomplish these objectives, they'll personally make a significant bonus, be in line for stock options, and likely be considered for a promotion, etc.... One level removed, it will allow them to do their part in working toward company growth.

But what's their challenge? What's keeping them from reaching those goals? Again, after working with so many for so long, I can almost read their mind when we're discussing this in person:

- (X) Their salespeople have trouble communicating the value of their premium-priced product or service, leading to a lower than acceptable closing ratio and a sales cycle that carries on way too long. Additionally, their salespeople typically aren't cross-selling into existing accounts for the same reason.

- (X) Due to a lack of effective onboarding, training, and coaching, it typically takes a new sales rep about twelve months to be fully productive by company standards, which is way too long.

They are not worried about putting my three kids through college. They're worried about putting *their* three kids through college.

After I've shared my Why Story, it would feel disingenuous to go straight into what I want them to buy. If I truly care about them—this new acquaintance that I've shared a part of my life story with and who's shared part of theirs—then what I'm there for is to help them solve their problems.

A Day in the Life of Your Customer

I've worked with plenty of salespeople in the wholesale financial services industry. Their customers are usually financial advisors—the person who sits across the desk or the kitchen table from Mr. and Mrs. Smith, trying to persuade them to invest their retirement portfolio in a certain investment vehicle. The wholesale reps are usually great at going in and bedazzling the financial advisors with their product knowledge and illustration navigation prowess, etc.... After all, that is their highest level of training so, naturally, they let it flow like a river.

"Okay," I said to one group of wholesalers. "But what's the financial advisor's problem? What's important to them? What are their goals, personally and professionally?"

I could tell they had never really thought about it quite like that before. I'm not knocking this particular group of professionals, but no one had ever challenged them to walk a mile in a financial advisor's shoes.

We did an exercise around **what a "day in the life" looks like for their customer, the advisor.**

"I'll tell you this: I seriously doubt they bounded out of bed this morning, shouting: 'Aw, man! Today's the day I get to meet the wholesale rep from Financial Rock! I can't wait!' That's not how they start the day," I pointed out.

Financial advisors have tremendous pressure to get new clients, all while worrying about losing the ones they have. If they have three prospect meetings, they're worried about what happens if they don't close them. They're worried about what to say to the two clients who left messages the night before saying that they're worried about what the market's doing. Are they going to jump ship?

While all of this is going on in their mind, they have an appointment with a financial wholesaler who's going to dump a load of information and new products that will take the advisor loads of time and energy to digest and determine if they should use that particular investment vehicle or not.

After going through a typical day, I said, "Now, with that mind-set, let's go back to the first question: What's important to them? What do they really care about? Are they really interested in learning about yet another life insurance product, mutual fund, or annuity?"

The insights from that exercise catalyzed an entirely new approach for these wholesalers. Instead of presenting a product, they now begin by talking about retention rates for high-net worth clients. They talk about how difficult it is to present financial vehicles in a way the layperson can understand. Then, they show the advisor how to lead an effective conversation in a simple, yet effective way proven to get more new clients to agree to hand over their hard-earned assets to their care.

Instead of focusing on features and benefits, they've reoriented their entire approach to focusing on solving the customer's problems that can prevent them from accomplishing their goals.

...just as you're going to learn how to do in chapter nine.

9

END WITH HOW:
THE 5 NEUROSELLING
NARRATIVES

RECENTLY, ONE OF my partners at Braintrust, who leads our client coaching program, received a call from one of our sales managers at a financial services client.

"Listen to what just happened to one of our reps," the manager said. "He had gone into an office with three advisors, but only one of them had time to meet him. He used a marker and a whiteboard to walk the advisor through the stories you helped us create with NeuroSelling. When the interactive whiteboard story was complete, the advisor erased the whiteboard, called one of the other partners in and said, 'Do that again!' So, the wholesaler sales rep grabbed the markers, headed to the whiteboard, and did the same story again. Amazingly, the second advisor went and got the third one, then sat down and said, 'Do it again!' I have *never* seen something quite like this approach!"

What did he do? Simple, really. He walked into the office with a solid understanding of what those advisors were really grappling with ("start with who"). Then he simply laid out the 5 "P" Stories:

- ✓ Personal story

- ✓ Prospect story

- ✓ Problem story

- ✓ Product/solution story

- ✓ Proof story

Throughout this book, I've talked about the importance of narratives. This chapter gets to the heart of NeuroSelling: How to take everything we've talked about up to this point and put it together in a sequence that leads to more urgency to "change" or buy. I'll first give you a high-level overview of each narrative or story followed by a deeper example of each.

Narrative #1 is your "Personal 'Why Story.'" You use this to *create a personal connection with your customer and invite them to share why they do what they do.* This drives personal trust higher and allows the prospect to lower their "self-preservation" defense shields.

In Narrative #2, the "Prospect story," you *create a story about the prospect that shows you understand their world and have a good handle on their overarching goals and objectives.* They are the main character in this story so gaining agreement and alignment on where they are trying to "go" shows you care about them and understand their business. This will also help establish your professional credibility while, at the same time, you demonstrate empathy to their situation which further reinforces the personal trust they already have in you that was established with your previous "why" story. In addition, this story serves to allow the prospect to agree, in their own words, to the "target" they are trying to hit.

Next, you will inject **Narrative #3, the "Problem story."** This story is designed to *introduce the antagonist or problem(s) preventing them from hitting their "targets" (i.e., goals and objectives) from the previous story.* If done correctly, the problem(s) will be associated with the threats and risks to their goals as well as the potential missed opportunities that are either currently or could potentially prevent them from reaching those goals or objectives. Designed within this story is also the need to *"quantify" the risk of not hitting the target.*

The best way to do this is by leveraging third-party insights to underscore the problem. For instance, if you are selling a CRM SaaS solution, you should know that my problem isn't just organizing and tracking the buyer journey and the internal sales process, as that is my goal or objective. My true problem lies in the potential cost of not doing that effectively.

If you told me that according to SBI nearly 60 percent of deals end in no decision then began asking me why I think that may be the case, what you should eventually uncover is that due to an inefficient, deal-flow tracking system, we are losing over 60 percent of the opportunities in our pipeline. If my average deal size is $20,000 and we are working 100 deals per month but are losing 60 percent of those deals, that's 60 deals lost per month × $20,000 per deal or $1.2 million in potential lost revenue...per month! That's your problem!

Now, how much worse will the problem be if they continue to sit on it? Remember: People don't change until the pain of staying the same becomes greater than the pain of change. You want to ensure they are fully aware of and own the pain of staying the same. This is accomplished by delivering an effective "problem" narrative.

That logically leads to **Narrative #4, the "Product/solution story,"** whereby *you solve the problem with your solution.* As their partner, the best thing you can do to serve them is to actually help them solve their problem.

It just so happens you're doing it with your own product or service. While delivering that narrative, you want to present why you're uniquely qualified to solve their issue. How do you describe your product or service in a simple and understandable way? How does your product or service work? What makes it different? How does it directly and quantifiably solve the problems you've been discussing? Answering these questions will help your prospect see the value of your solution with clarity and simplicity.

With **Narrative #5, the "Proof story,"** you want to give information for their neocortex that validates what their limbic and root brains already feel. *Present a narrative about customers like them who used your product and experienced the results.*

These customer testimonials or "validation" stories ensure the prospect that they aren't alone. It reduces the cortisol and minimizes the potential perception of risk associated with change.

That's the quick-and-dirty version to give you a road map of what we're doing in this chapter.

Here's the secret sauce—by following this order of stories, you are providing information to your prospect in the way *and* the order that their brain likes to naturally process that information in order to make a decision to change.

If you skip a step or get your narratives out of order, you will likely trigger areas in their brain that will either cause their defense shields to go up or eject from the process entirely and head back for status quo.

Now, let's dive deeper into the "how" by walking through an example of each narrative, connected together and wrapped around a specific example.

Our prospect, Jim, is the EVP of sales for a large enterprise software company. As you read through this overarching sales conversation, simply picture your ideal prospect and begin to see how transferrable these narratives can be in your world. Let's say we sell sales enablement, coaching, and training. Let's take these narratives one by one, starting with Narrative Two.

The Personal Story

Perhaps one of the greatest acceptance speeches I've ever witnessed was Fred "Won't You Be My Neighbor?" Rogers accepting a lifetime achievement award at the twenty-fourth annual Daytime Emmy Awards.

He said, "So many people have helped me to this night. Some of you are here. Some are far away. Some are even in Heaven. All of us have special ones who have loved us into being. Would you just take, along with me, ten seconds to think of the people who have helped you become who you are? Those who have cared about you and wanted what was best for you in life? Ten seconds of silence; I'll watch the time."

After a beautiful stretch of silence—many in the audience with tears in their eyes—our beloved Mr. Rogers continued: "Whomever you've been thinking about, how pleased they must be to know the difference you feel they've made."

Go watch the video. It's worth every second of your time.

Now, I ask you: Who did you think about? Who was someone you looked up to and respected? Who invested some time in your life and made a difference? They're probably your sage.

In my workshops, the Sage has often been a parent or grandparent, but just as often, I've seen others, like an uncle, a foster mother, a band teacher, an older sibling, a minister, a family friend. It doesn't matter. They only have to matter to you.

On the flip side, **a great Why Story is *belief*-centric, not *me*-centric.**

We don't want to hear about how great you are and how you were the hero of your own tale.

If Christina would have told a story about how she picked herself up by the bootstraps and how strong she was now, her story wouldn't have had nearly the same effect. In her story, her future husband and the leadership program were the real heroes. Matt's story wasn't about him, but about his sweet, thoughtful mother and the lessons she instilled. My airplane buddy's story was mostly about his grandpa. My own story isn't about how great Jeff Bloomfield is, but how great Papaw Bloomfield was. These characters are the hinges the rest of the story turns on.

I like to call them "The Sage." Just about every great story has a wise old man or woman who helps the hero. Luke Skywalker had Obi-Wan Kenobi and then Yoda. Bilbo and then Frodo had the wizard Gandalf. Queen Ester had Mordecai. Dorothy had Glinda, the Good Witch of the North. The Sage is the person bringing the hero wisdom and inspiring them to do something different.

So, **Element #1:** *It cannot be about how great you, the narrator, are.* The change or call to action has to come from somewhere beyond you. It cannot be me-centric.

Element #2: *It must be belief centric.* It isn't really about the narrator; it's about the listener. In my Why Story, I share four beliefs I learned from Papaw: hard work/perseverance, problem-solving, the platinum rule, and the importance of family.

Let me ask you a question: Do you believe all four of those beliefs are important? Likely, you do. I have yet to meet someone who doesn't either share or at minimum, agree with those beliefs. No one would say that they *didn't* believe in family or in treating people well, etc.... These are universal beliefs.

Remember: *To universally connect with people, it's critical to display beliefs that are universally relatable.*

Everybody can connect with my airplane friend's belief that you should do what's right, even when nobody's looking. Everybody can believe in Matt's mother's message about walking in someone else's shoes. You don't want to share beliefs that aren't universally accepted, especially the polarizing topics of religion and politics.

Alienating people is the opposite of what you're trying to do.

There's nothing wrong with having core beliefs based around your religious or political affiliations; I do myself. They just *aren't very likely to be universal* and, in fact, have around a 50 percent chance to actually turn the person against you instead of connecting you. And keep in mind, from a neuroscientific standpoint, this story is designed to allow your prospect to quickly move you from the "foe" or potential foe category to the relatable, possible friend category. It helps you seem less "risky."

Now, think about what you believe. What core values do you truly hold deep down? The kind of beliefs that unite us and form the bedrock of how you've built your life. You may not realize it, but we are united in our beliefs far more than we are different. The problem is that we don't always live out those beliefs, so people are used to being hurt. Getting burned. But when someone reminds us of just how united we are, it restores our own beliefs again and reminds us of the good in others.

Here are just a few common beliefs I've seen in others' Why Stories:

- ✓ Choosing love, especially when it was hard

- ✓ Patience being rewarded

- ✓ Doing the right thing, no matter what

- ✓ Helping others, even if it meant sacrifice

- ✓ Doing a job well, even it meant doing it again

- ✓ Doing more than expected

- ✓ The Golden Rule (or Platinum Rule in my case)

- ✓ The importance of family

- ✓ Being kind, even to a "nobody"

- ✓ Problem-solvers rule the world

You have beliefs like this, even if it's been a long time since you thought about them. You expect people to act a certain way or you believe that there is a right way. When people don't behave that certain way, it probably makes you angry or upset. You believe there is a way the world ought to be.

Figure out what those beliefs are for you.

Now, put Elements #1 and #2 together:

How did your sage help you learn those beliefs? It can be directly or even by observing the way they lived their life.

How did you see your beliefs reflected in their actions and life? Try to think about a specific time or a recurring event.

Matt's mother took him and his brother to the homeless kitchen every Saturday—that was what "sacrificing for others" looked like. Him giving away the shoes he and his mother had saved for to a homeless man was "empathy" manifested.

When you think of those specific times, *the third element of a great Why Story should come almost naturally*—**visual anchors.**

When I'm making my point about hard work and perseverance, I talk about going on the tractor back and forth between the rows of our fields. The visual cue for problem-solving is duct tape. The Platinum Rule looks like my Papaw returning Old Man Crouse's red pickup truck with a full tank of gas. **Each belief has a visual that my listener can see in their mind's eye.**

When you have your three elements down, the final act is to tie it all together:

1. The transition: why you're about to tell the listener a story quite different than they're used to

   "Before we jump into today's agenda, I'd like to take just two minutes to tell you why I do what I do, then I'd love to hear why you do what you do, okay?"

2. The scene: transport the listener to the place your story takes place

   "I grew up on a one-hundred-acre farm in north central Ohio. My papaw bought that farm with his life savings, having moved

the family up from Kentucky when my dad was just a boy. It was on this farm that I learned most of the lessons that make me who I am today."

3. The narrative: tell your story

   "I can still remember learning how to drive when I just five years old..."

4. The bridge: the logical conclusion of how your Why Story is relevant to helping the listener

   "So, today I love helping others learn how to apply these techniques in the way they build and deliver their message. Turns out, it helps just as much at home as it does with prospects and customers!"

5. The end: an intentional statement to invite them to share their Why Story

   "That's why I do what I do. How about you? Why do you do what you do?"

It really is that straightforward.

Simple...just not easy but once you get it "built," you can customize it for any situation.

Here's an **example of a Why Story from one of our** NeuroSelling **graduates** at a financial services client, Ben Robertson. I'd like you to read it as if you're the customer and Ben is telling it to you as a way to begin an otherwise high-pressured sales meeting. Then I'd like you to ask yourself, "do I trust this guy?"

> *"Before we get into the agenda today, I'd like to take just a moment to tell you why I do what I do, then I'd love to hear why you do what you do. Growing up in a traditional, southern family, our*

particular clan was run by a strong patriarch, Otis Kelly Robertson, or as I knew him, Granddad. Granddad grew up in Hazard, Kentucky. I used to always get a kick out of him telling me the way he gave directions to his house was "head to the first holler, turn at the second creek. The white house with all the chickens." Granddad believed in three things; Faith, Family, and Fishing. All my earliest childhood memories were on the water. Every free weekend, summer vacation, and day off school was spent with Granddad at the lake.

He would always have these sayings that I thought were only about fishing, but as I grew up, I have learned were his way of teaching me valuable life lessons. The first was, "You catch your first fish the night before." I can vividly remember him in the garage the night before we were going to the lake putting new fishing line on poles, tying on different lures, checking the oil in the boat, all to make sure that when we hit the water in the morning, nothing would hinder our ability to immediately start fishing. In other words, the right preparation for something important can be the difference between success and failure, not just in fishing, but in life. He also frequently reminded me that "You should always know where all the stumps and rocks are." When you're fishing, hidden structures in the water such as stumps and rocks can be your best friend because fish live and hang out near them. But they can also be your worst enemy if you hit one with your boat you didn't know was there while driving down the lake. Knowing your obstacles and learning to use them to your advantage can be the difference in catching your biggest fish of the day or putting a hole in the side of your boat.

He also taught me that "Boaters take care of boaters when you're on the water." If you aren't a fisherman you may not know this but pleasure boaters (jet skis, tubers and skiers) aren't always well liked by the fishing community. When the sun comes up and it starts to get hot on a summer day, what started out as a quiet, calm cove can turn into a loud and wavy spring-break style-party pretty quickly. Granddad would always just shake his head and curse under his breath as the jet ski flew by way too close to our boat. But one day while heading back into the boat ramp just before dark, we passed a large ski boat full of younger-looking guys floating in the middle of a main channel, clearly stranded. Their engine had given out and they were adrift. Granddad didn't hesitate to help. He hooked up a tow rope and towed the boys' boat back into the dock. When you're on the water, all boaters are equal, and we must take care of each other. The financial services industry is like the boating community and keeping the Golden Rule in mind is paramount. We need each other to succeed.

These life lessons helped shape me into the man I am today and guide my mission with advisors like you every day. Coaching my customers on proper preparation so they hit the water ready to fish, educating them on the obstacles they may run into, and showing them how to turn those same potential obstacles into opportunities, while always remembering to take care of others in our industry is why I get out of bed every day. That's why I do what I do.

Now, why do you do what you do?"

How do you think most of his prospects and customers respond to that story? You guessed it...extremely well. They generally launch into their own story about their dad, grandpa, mom, aunt, or other strong influencer in their life who taught them similar beliefs. Please don't think that this type of story is unnecessary. The science would dictate otherwise. It's a fast lane to personal trust.

For those of you who may want to see the "elevator"-pitch style of this story, here's the condensed version:

"Before we jump straight into the agenda today, I'd like to take just a minute to share why I do what I do, then I'd love to hear why you do what you do. I was raised in the south and come from a long line of fishermen. My granddad, Otis Robertson, was the patriarch of all patriarchs and the captain of every fishing adventure I went on as a boy. He taught me three things on those adventures that I still value today and believe will have relevance to our conversation in just a bit. First, he taught me that you actually catch the first fish the night before. Success in fishing (and life) can be found in the preparation. The more prepared you are, the better your odds of landing the big one.

Next, he taught me that stumps and rocks can be your best friend or your worst enemy. These hidden structures are where the fish tend to hang out but if you don't know they are there, they can also sink your boat. The lesson? See what others don't see and learn how to take what others see as obstacles and turn them into opportunities.

Finally, he taught me that you should always be willing to help a fellow boater as you'll never know when you, yourself might need the help. Who would have thought all those years ago that the lessons I was learning on that lake would allow me to one day help people like you grow their practices and that's really why I do what I do. How about you? Why do you do what you do?"

The first version, the "extended cut," has more detail and can be used when you have more time. That version generally takes between two to three minutes. The second version, the "condensed why," can usually be told in a minute or less. The key for your "why" story is to have a full version and then several iterations that can be used at the right time for the right environment.

Guess what? Your "why" story isn't just for sales. It can also be used as a coach and a leader going for the next promotion! When I worked with Kevin, he was the equivalent of an Executive Vice President or General Manager for the Midwest market of a large enterprise client. Like just about everyone in sales, he was trained from a traditional standpoint: sales was a transaction to be had, not a relationship to be made. But NeuroSelling rang true with him and he invested his time and energy in learning it.

We worked together around a year with his team. About six months after our first engagement ended, he invited me to lunch. When we sat down at the restaurant, he said, "This is my treat."

"Thank you!" I said. "Wow, what for?"

He said, "I've just been promoted to CEO. It hasn't been announced yet, but I wanted to share the story with you because my Why Story played a central role in getting me the job.

"The hiring process was pretty rigorous. It came down to me and two other candidates. Really, they were way more qualified and had much more experience than I did. For the final phase, they submitted a list of questions for all of us to answer, followed by a final interview with each of us about our answers.

"Instead of just submitting my answers, I hired a professional videographer and recorded my Why Story. After I told my Why Story, toward the end, I went through each of the questions and answered them how they were probably expecting. Then I submitted the video instead of a written response."

In my head, I was thinking, *Man, I already see where this is going!*

Kevin said, "When we got to the live interview panel, we each had ninety minutes." He paused. "But I only got thirty minutes to answer the original questions."

"What?! Why?" I asked, completely thrown off. I'd expected him to say that it'd gone on for longer—not shorter!

"Well," he said, "because the first sixty minutes was essentially each person on the panel sharing their own personal experiences and talking about how my story resonated with them on such a deep level. Toward the end, they said, 'Oh, yeah, we know you answered the other questions. Just give us a little color around a couple of things...' Then we just ran through a few things, almost like an afterthought. Yeah, everybody told me I had the longest shot out of all three of us, but here I am!"

Later, Kevin found out through the grapevine that the other two interviews had gone very differently, more of a "just the facts, ma'am" interview.

I share this story to point out that NeuroSelling isn't just about selling. Sure, that's a practical application, but it's really a communication model. Whether you're "influencing" someone to hire you, getting a child to eat their vegetables, or showing a customer a new way of thinking, you need to connect with others on a personal level.

We've covered quite a bit of ground so far, but we have much further to go. We've really only touched on the elements needed to create that opening "personal trust." We still need to work on using the model to drive that urgency to change that moves you from the Tommy Boy quadrant on the trust matrix up to the Matt Rogers quadrant. Now, it's time to start seeing how this science can further help you sell.

Remember: *Start with who.*

The Prospect Story

Always keep in mind, from your prospect's perspective, you're walking into their world, their "safety box" and, telling them that they need to change. Essentially, you're telling them they've been doing it wrong, but lucky for them, you're there like a masked superhero to save the day!

You're not there to be their knight in shining armor. You're there to help narrate a set of problems they're already likely working through or possibly aren't aware of but should be, and then narrate how the future *could* look if the two of you partnered together to solve them. Ultimately, your goal is to make *them* the hero of their own story, not you.

First, we need to make sure that we're talking about the things your customer cares about, this is his or her story after all. Let's revisit our example whereby we are selling sales enablement, coaching, and training programs. You've already opened with your personal story so now the "Prospect story" could go something like this with our executive prospect, Jim:

> *"Jim, as I was driving in today, I was thinking about all the pressure that must be on your shoulders. I swung into the Shell station to get gas and decided to get something to drink while I was there. I opened the cooler door to the bottles of water section at the back of the store only to be greeted by seven rows of various brands of water, all with different price points. I quickly scanned up and down and grabbed the "2 for 1" special and made my way back to my truck and headed down the road. As I glanced down at my cup holder, I noticed I had a different empty bottle of water left over from the day before sitting alongside my new bottle from today. The only difference was the label and the color of the lid. Pretty hard to tell them apart. I then realized that on both days, at separate gas stations, I had chosen the least expensive bottle of water each time."*

(Pause) Notice, I didn't barge into the room, telling the customer what they were doing wrong. Captain Kirk would have instantly raised shields and Mr. Spock would have begun quickly refuting and negating everything I threw at them. Instead, I told them a story (in this case, using an analogy) they could relate to. Without hard facts to refute, Mr. Spock pipes down and Captain Kirk leans in, wondering where I'm going with this story. Curiosity and relatability are magical ingredients to every great

story. The power is in their hands. They get to come to their own conclusion without me trying to pull them into it.

> *"That brings me to you. I have the privilege of working with several CEOs, presidents, and VPs of sales and marketing. When we discuss their top three or four high-level objectives, it's striking how similar they are. #1: Increase top line revenue; #2: Improve profitability by reducing the amount of discounting required to secure new business; #3: Shorten the time it takes to get deals completed through the pipeline (sales cycle); and #4: Shorten the time it takes to get new salespeople trained and producing results. Jim, do any or all of those goals resonate with what you are working on today?"*

(If we've done our homework, we should never be wrong with these goals, no matter what business you're in).

> *"Jim, tell me what your actual targeted goals are for each—i.e. how much of an increase in revenue are you trying to achieve as a company? How do you currently measure the impact discounting has on your business? What's your average current sales cycle time? What would you like it to be? Finally, do you measure the time it currently takes to get your new reps trained and productive? How much improvement would you like to see here...weeks? Months?"*

(The above will be a natural, back-and-forth conversation. You are simply getting Jim to tell you his perspective on the "targets," how he measures the targets, etc.... This will allow you to properly put those targets at risk with your upcoming problem story.)

I'll take a quick pause here from our Prospect story to show you what we just accomplished. We used a story to introduce the Prospect story with the bottle of water narrative. You will soon see where I'm headed with that story.

Suffice to say, Jim doesn't know either, but he's likely curious.

Next, we mentioned that we work with people just like him (empathy, credibility) and then proceeded to tell him what his peers stated were their typical top three or four goals.

The secret sauce is *picking high enough level goals that resonate with your prospect but aligned in a way that allows you to eventually position a problem that you can solve.*

We then asked Jim to help us understand how he currently measures those goals. This gives you tremendous insight into how Jim sees his world and the added bonus of staying completely on his agenda.

You have essentially told him a story about himself and allowed him to participate in the details of that story as the main character. When you feel like you're participating in the development of a story, you become even more invested in the outcome being a happy ending! (See choice-supportive bias in chapter six). Now that you've set the table nicely with the Prospect story, it's time to introduce the antagonist to our main character's goals, the "Problem story."

The Problem Story

The easiest action is always inaction. This next step is a crucial link in persuading your customer that they have a problem they really need to do something about.

As we said earlier, your biggest competitor isn't the competition—it's indecision.

Your job is to create urgency to take action by juxtaposing your prospect's current goals against the very antagonist that can or likely may already be preventing them from accomplishing said goals.

At this point in the conversation, it's tempting to launch into the full array of what you offer and how it can help them. But the moment you present anything, Grug Crood is going to rear his ugly head: "This is new. New is bad. Grug no change!"

The moment you introduce anything new, you're telling your customer that they need to leave their safety box. Nobody wants to leave their safety box. Even if it's smelly, dank, and leaks when it rains, we feel safe there.

Before talking about their future (with you), you have to make them understand why their present isn't tenable.

They need to come to their own conclusion that the pain of staying the same outweighs the perceived pain of change.

Grug Crood didn't leave his cave until an earthquake destroyed it. He left because he had to, not because he wanted to. In fact, a smart kid tried to tell him that an earthquake was coming and Grug wouldn't listen. His family had to have a near-death experience before he finally set out in search of something better. Your job in this next step is to get Grug to see that an earthquake's a-comin'.

Now, remember that you want your customers to have a little spike of cortisol. It focuses their attention on the problem and the insight you're providing.

It's easy: *All you have to do is remind them of the fear they already have. Just show them that status quo is not an option.*

I structure my problem narratives around four Is:

- ✓ **Issue** (problem(s), prioritized)

- ✓ **Impact** (quantifiable cost of the problem)

- ✓ **Invasiveness** (the larger, organizational impact of the problem)

- ✓ **Iceberg** (the giant barrier that has prevented them from solving it thus far)

First, we need agreement around the primary issue they're facing. In fact, they need to verbalize it. Once the words are out of their mouth, they own the problem. Of course, they're facing multiple problems, usually. They need to set the priority.

Traditional selling has you present the problem, then get the customer to agree that it is a problem. With NeuroSelling, *you're building the seeds of partnership because they're "confessing" what their real problems are in their own words.*

Second, you need to *quantify the impact of that issue.*

I cannot stress this enough: You need to quantify the impact.

Remember: *the fear of loss is twice as motivating as the possibility of gain.*

Their problem starts to get real when you begin putting pen to paper. What is the quantifiable impact of indecision, a.k.a. the status quo? We're telling Grug that his safety box isn't safe at all. We're spiking his cortisol so that he sees the danger of doing nothing.

In NeuroSelling lingo, we're resetting his anchor point for the solution we're about to present.

His anchor point of comparison can't be about the price of your solution. Instead, he needs to view the investment of the solution against the cost of the inevitable problem. Let's continue the story...

> *"Jim, I'm one of those nerds who love reading. I read nearly anything I can get my hands on, particularly when it relates to business and important trends that affect my clients. Recently, I was reading the "State of Sales" report that Salesforce puts out each year. It reported that almost 60 percent of sales reps will miss their quota. Further, Sirius Decisions reported that in a survey to sales executives like yourself, the Number One reason sales reps miss quota is their inability to articulate value in the customer conversation. This data makes sense why CEB found that 86 percent of customers reported not being able to see a difference from one supplier (salesperson) and their competitor. As a result, the Global Chief Sales Officer study reported sales cycles are getting longer in 64 percent of companies!*

So, back to my original bottle of water story from earlier. Here's the crux of the issue: Companies today struggle to meet revenue goals, discount way too often, and as a result, elongate their sales cycle because the salespeople can't effectively differentiate themselves and create value in the customer conversation. Period. And as a result of that, your customers view your salespeople the way I viewed those bottles of water in that gas station cooler. Simply the same bottles with a different label. And when you view something as the same, you don't see value and when you don't see value, you either don't choose at all or choose the lowest price. Does any of this seem to resonate with your world today?"

Next, to help make the problems concrete, drive just the right amount of cortisol to help Jim focus his attention and create urgency to change, we need to help him "quantify" the real, tangible cost of this problem to him.

"Jim, earlier you mentioned the company has a 20 percent revenue increase goal. What was the average quota for your reps last year?"

"$1 million/rep."

"Okay, so that means this year, the average quota is around $1.2 million, correct?"

"Yes, that's about right, give or take."

"And how many reps do you currently have?"

"One hundred."

"Okay, so you have one hundred reps, all of which need to increase their sales by $200,000 each, correct?"

"Yes".

"Well, if my farmboy math is correct, it sounds like you have a $200K per rep problem and a $20 million company problem to solve."

You get the idea, right? By putting a cost to the status quo and chunking it down to a per-line problem, the neocortex isn't comparing your price against the cost of doing nothing (which we always think is zero dollars). Instead, you've activated the fear/risk of loss. In this case, the risk of losing somewhere in the neighborhood of $200K per rep if every rep stays at the past year's sales performance.

In reality, you and I know performance always happens on a bell curve, so the reality is likely somewhere in the middle. But here's the beautiful thing, whatever Jim tells you is still a much higher anchor than the likely cost of your solution!

What if he says, "Well...most of our reps will be somewhere between 100 and 120 percent to plan. Okay, then let's settle in at 110 percent. That means each rep grew by, on average, $100,000. That still leaves Jim with a $100K/rep problem. Unless you are selling a solution that costs over $100K per person, you have created contrast.

Grug's cave is caving in!

We've covered the first two Is: the issue and the impact.

Now, we need to take it one step further and talk about invasiveness: What's the broader cost of the status quo? Is the problem worse than they think?

Most customers—and, subsequently, most salespeople—focus primarily on the impact the issue/problem has on their direct job or department. That's a myopic view. Every part of an organization is linked. **Every action has a ripple effect.**

I like to invite the customer to think more broadly:

- What's going to happen if things don't change?

- What happens if production continues to bleed $20 million?

- What's the impact to other departments if the sales team doesn't hit its quota?

- In other words, how invasive is this problem?

By asking them what the broader organizational implications are, it underscores the urgency of the situation and just how big of a problem it really is.

And again, **these are their words—not yours.**

For example, if they don't hit their growth goals, what gets cut? Where does the leadership find the extra profitability? Do they lay off people? Cut R&D? Reduce bonuses? All of these are invasive "ripple" effects of the problem from an organizational standpoint.

Now, let's continue the "quantification" of the problem to further drive urgency to change.

"When it comes to the discounting problem, what's your current average deal size?"

"$10,000."

"And what's your average discounting rate across the sales org?"

"Typically, we end up seeing around a 10 percent discount to get the business."

"Okay, so again, if my math is correct, If my sales goal is $1.2 million, that's normally 120 deals at $10K per deal. However, if I'm discounting 10 percent, I'll need to sell 12 additional deals just

to produce the same amount of revenue. Essentially, discounting alone is another $120,000 problem. Did I do my math right?"

"Wow, you really do think about this from every angle, Jeff!"

"I know what it's like to be in your shoes and I know that even small, positive changes can be the difference between making the number and being a hero to the board of directors or missing the number and being the goat."

You see, you don't need to hype up the problem. If you walk them through the scenario to its logical conclusion, they can see for themselves the true gravity of their problem.

Fourth and last of the "Is", is the "Iceberg":

What obstruction/barrier has kept them from solving the problem to this point? I can almost guarantee you that it comes down to one of these:

1. The know-how (expertise) to solve it

2. The time to devote to solving it

3. The resources (in people or money) needed to solve it

When you understand what's preventing them from solving the issue, you're likely to uncover a list of change barriers they were subconsciously thinking about. (And don't fret: We have a whole chapter devoted to handling these barriers coming up.)

It's important to ask this question to determine what they have been doing to try to solve the problem prior to your conversation.

Maybe they've been doing nothing. Maybe they've been using a competitor. Maybe they've been trying to do something with their internal team. Either way, it's important for you to know this as it's part of their current status quo and will be what they will have to move away from in order to move toward you!

Now, let's take another break to review.

At this point:

- ✓ You've told your personal Why Story to create personal trust.

- ✓ You then crafted and delivered a compelling Prospect story and allowed them to participate in the creation of that story.

- ✓ You then pivoted using third-party insights to deliver a compelling problem story that puts their current goals and objectives at significant risk.

- ✓ By then quantifying the actual cost of the problem, you now have a significant "anchor" point to work from later when you present your solution and price.

In the end, if salespeople can't drive urgency to change with value clarity in the customer conversation, then you'll end up discounting far too often, elongate the sales cycle, and ultimately miss your revenue goals.

Wow.

That's a lot of ground to cover but we've allowed Jim to feel in complete control of the agenda since we've only discussed the things he cares about and the problems that could prevent his goals.

The key to remember here is we didn't open the call up with the dreaded "twenty questions"…We came armed with knowledge about Jim and *we* controlled the narrative, and yet Jim still felt in complete control!

Now that we've established the primary problem that needs to be solved for Jim and his organization (sales team effectiveness) we can move on to story #4, the "Product/Solution story".

The Product/Solution Story

Alright, here's where you get to show off your vast reservoir of credibility. You get to use all the features and benefits you've worked so hard to memorize, the stuff all your presentations and pitches are made of! Finally!

...right?

Of course not.

We're using neuroscience here. We know that the brain can only process so much information before it gets overwhelmed and shuts down. Your customer doesn't care about your product or service. They care about being the hero of their own story. So, paint that picture for them *and nothing else.*

Don't try to unload all the bells and whistles and everything you could possibly do for them.

Those conversations come later. Right now, you need to be laser-focused on bridging the gap between where they are and where they want to be.

> It's important to always keep in mind as you prepare for any customer conversation that, in the end, if you don't put yourself in a position to solve the problem with your product or solution, none of the earlier narratives do you much good!

In our case at Braintrust, we have programs that leverage the science of customer decision-making to help salespeople develop trust quicker and create customer conversations that drive urgency to change. That's NeuroSelling in a nutshell. And it's just what the doctor ordered for a client like Jim. Let's dive into the "Product/Solution story."

"Jim, I understand that changing the way your salespeople communicate can seem like a herculean task. After all, over the years you've likely tried any number of various sales training and coaching programs, correct? Do you have any idea why most of

them never seem to stick? Usually, it's for two reasons. Number One, these programs typically focus on helping you talk more about you. Guess what? Your customer doesn't care about you. They care about themselves! And Two, in order to effectively drive willingness to change in another human being, your customer in this case, you have to understand the science of human decision-making. You have to communicate the right information at just the right time and in the right order.

You see, the past couple of decades have brought about neuroscience research that has illuminated how the human brain processes information in order to make a decision. Turns out, the vast majority of sales and marketing professionals communicate with their customer's brain in a way that's not only counterproductive to the way it likes to process information, but also their message typically drives skepticism, defensiveness, and doubt! The exact opposite of what you're trying to accomplish! Now that we've cracked the code on the decision-making process, we can use the biology, psychology, and physiology to create and deliver messaging that drives trust faster while, at the same time, creates urgency to change. Does this sound like the type of program you'd like to hear more about?"

From here, you can go into as much detail as Jim would like to see relative to how the program works, how it gets implemented, the supporting coaching, how it gets measured etc....

With the problem defined by him and quantified by you, there's just the iceberg question: What barrier exists today that would prevent him from doing something innovative and creative to ensure his salespeople hit or even exceed the goal? His answer becomes the frame for the solution you're about to offer.

For Braintrust, that narrative might go something like this:

"Jim, our sales enablement program—NeuroSelling—takes a scientific approach to the customer conversation. By following our methodology, your reps will connect quicker, build trust more effectively, and create an urgency to change on the part of your prospects.

Today, your reps are likely following a model similar to this: build rapport, ask probing questions to uncover pain, present a solution, handle objections, and close. The problem? This model forces the conversation into the wrong part of your prospect's brain. In fact, it actually speaks to the skeptical brain.

What if you could teach them how the buying brain works and then give them a repeatable model to create clear differentiation from your competitors every time?

The NeuroSelling method uses the knowledge of the buying brain to build a customer conversation around connection first, then credibility by using insight and visual narratives to create clear, compelling differentiation and urgency to buy. We take advantage of the six "limbic levers" of emotion, visualization, experience, contrast, simplicity, and egocentricity to ensure the narrative your reps deliver paint a clear buying vision and a need to solve the problem at hand immediately.

This way, reps see an immediate impact in their ability to create trust and, as a result, see their closing ratios go up and the need to discount go down. As you can imagine, this significantly impacts revenue and shortens sales cycles as well."

In this narrative, notice I didn't talk about other programs we offer, NeuroMessaging or NeuroCoaching. I didn't talk about our storyboarding solutions. I didn't try to tell him everything Braintrust could possibly do for his company. I addressed the problem he said was important to him.

Also note that **the narrative isn't about what Braintrust was going to do for him.** I didn't want to engage his skeptical neocortex. I wanted to speak to his welcoming limbic system and root brain. I want *him* to paint the picture in his mind. I want *his brain* to picture himself as the hero.

I want him to sell himself.

Now that we've properly peppered the root brain and limbic system, we have to allow Jim's neocortex to participate and "validate" the way he feels in order to justify moving forward.

The Proof Story

I can't tell you how many customer testimonials and case studies I've read that were just a collection of facts and figures: "Customer X used our services. They achieved a reduction in cost of $Y or Z%. Hooray us. It could have been so much more effective structured as a simple narrative.

Again, the neuroscience we're relying on with the Proof story is that we know the neocortex needs to "activate" at some point in order to justify and validate the feelings we've created in our first four stories. To do that, we are going to initially bypass the neocortex and activate the limbic system and root brain with the story. Since the narrative we'll be using is happening to someone else, there's no threat to the prospect. You're not asking their neocortex to accept or reject anything you're telling them. A story doesn't invite judgment and scrutiny like facts and figures do.

You're not asking them to change or do anything, so their self-preservation orientation doesn't trigger.

When I start reading or hearing a properly constructed testimonial story, my brain immediately pictures what's happening, automatically conjuring images and scenes as my internal visualization mechanism starts up. Without even being aware of it, I create an emotional attachment as my brain attempts to empathize with what I'm reading. It's why a great book can make us cry or feel fear: We're in the story with Wilbur as Charlotte spins her web or Frodo as the Nazgûl hunt for him and the Ring.

Customer validation stories are made for the NeuroSelling methodology. What if instead of a dry, factual recount of what happened to a client or customer of yours, it was couched in narrative form? That's how we'll deliver **Narrative #5: The Proof Story.**

> *"Let me take just a moment and tell you about my friend Larry. I'll never forget the first day I met with him. The air conditioning in his building was broken. It was July, so it was ninety-five degrees in his office. We ended up going out to the patio by their cafeteria just to get some air. We were both sweating profusely, and it wasn't because either of us was nervous!*
>
> *After we shared our Why Stories, he confided in me that they were behind again in their sales numbers and, as the VP, he was starting to feel the heat. He had risen to the rank of VP from a sales rep himself and just couldn't figure out how to get others to sell the way he used to. They had tried several tactics from internal boot camps on selling skills to even bringing in an outside consultant last year, but nothing seemed to be sticking. As it turned out, Larry needed to increase each rep's top-line output by an average of $200,000. That may not sound like a*

lot by itself but multiply that by the 200 reps they had and you can see just how daunting a $40 million problem was to Larry.

I shared with him that he certainly wasn't alone and that the Number One obstacle most companies were having to sales growth was their sales team's inability to tell an effective story that showed differentiation and value. The reason was simple but not easy.

Salespeople don't understand how the brain actually did things like build connection, trust, and ultimately make a buying decision. We walked through NeuroSelling just like you and I have today. He was tired of simply holding manager's meetings and trying to get them to be better "coaches." That was part of it, but not enough.

He had a decision to make and seeing how minimal the investment was compared to the potential that this program could have on his sales team and his sales culture, it seemed like the perfect solution.

We engaged his sales team the very next month, starting with the managers. And over the course of the next six months got all two hundred reps through our program.

One year later, the sales team had posted a collective $50 million increase in sales, year-over-year. Not only did we help Larry hit his number, but we also exceeded it by ten million dollars!

Needless to say, today Larry is one of our raving fans and has even embedded our program into the rep onboarding training and he's seeing faster productivity than ever before."

After reading that, do those numbers feel more compelling embedded in a narrative? Is it more convincing and compelling than saying "Yeah, we worked with this company one time. Got their sales reps to sell an extra $50 million."

No context, no connection.

But when it's time to talk about how much your product or service costs, that's where things get rough. Right? Not when you follow the NeuroSelling narratives laid out in this chapter.

Think about it from our prospect example, Jim's perspective. You know you've tried every "sales training du jour" over the years and you've gotten, at best, modest results. You also believe in this approach. What would you pay to help bridge the problem gap of somewhere between $100,000–$200,000 per rep? Would you pay $10,000 per rep? $20,000? Either sound pretty darn good compared to the cost of the problem now, don't they? When it comes to presenting pricing, most salespeople flinch as they slide the "napkin" across the table because they've been beaten down by so many customers in the past. They have a form of posttraumatic pricing presentation syndrome. I don't mean to sound harsh but it's likely your own fault.

Sorry to be so blunt **but when you haven't created contrast and shown differentiation with value clarity, why wouldn't I ask you for a discount?** Why wouldn't I compare you to the cheapest competitor on the market? You're a bottle of water, after all. Why should I pay more?

Good news is, you're a NeuroSelling salesperson now. You've done such a great job of using the "P" narratives that you've built personal trust and driven significant credibility alongside an urgency to solve the problem. It doesn't matter what you sell. The vast majority of our clients are the premium-priced solution in their given industry.

Using NeuroSelling you have the prospect *wanting* to choose you without as much concern over the investment as they know the value they are receiving. What a refreshing place to be.

Now that you have the foundation of the stories necessary to drive change using the NeuroSelling communication approach, over the next couple of chapters we will help you work through how to ask effective questions throughout the customer conversation as well as how to remove any remaining barriers to change. Your Jedi communication mastery is almost complete.

For Access to Free Bonus Tools to Help You Implement
the Concepts of NeuroSelling, go to:

www.braintrustgrowth.com/neurosellingtools

ASKING NEUROCENTRIC QUESTIONS

> *"The art and science of asking questions*
> *is the source of all knowledge."*
> —Thomas Berger, American novelist

WE ADOPTED OUR youngest daughter, Priya, from India when she was two-and-a-half-years old. After she began to get acclimated to her new surroundings, I was reminded of how powerful the curiosity of a toddler can be. However, it didn't take long to realize that her curiosity was different than my older two.

When Grace and Drew were toddlers, they asked questions that most secure, suburban toddlers ask: "Why does the dog have fur and I don't?" "Why does the moon shine at night but not during the day like the sun?" "Why do you yell at the TV when you're watching football?" You know, *those* types of questions.

But with Priya, her questions came from a different place. "Will you promise to sleep with me all night and not get up?" "When will mommy be home? She will be home, right?" Her questions were from a point of survival...of fear. As she became more and more secure and realized the safety of her new environment, she slowly began to ask questions that showed more curiosity than fear.

As we've covered in multiple places in this book, **as humans, our default setting is self-preservation orientation.** Not until we feel safe are we open to new ideas. Even when we think about asking effective questions, we have to understand that since we are under stress, you will tend to operate more with a self-serving perspective, even a survival mentality, than one of empathy and concern for the person of whom you are asking the question. When you are worried about your own survival or in this case, the survival of your sale, you tend to ask questions that are leading and noticeably on your agenda as opposed to your customer's agenda.

Most executives I speak with or we work with recognize the need for their sales team to act as consultants and sell "solutions" instead of products; but many CEOs and sales leaders are actually shocked at how poorly their sales teams execute on what they thought was supposed to be a "customer-centric" selling approach.

Recently, I had a conversation with an executive who was sitting next to me on a plane ride to the west coast. The subject of sales and sales effectiveness came up. It may not surprise you that at one point he said: "I can always tell when a rep has been through sales training, because instead of launching straight into a product pitch, they launch into a list of questions." Admittedly, he knew all too well that neither is the right approach.

Too often, sales teams trying to execute on what they believe is customer-centric, consultative selling never move beyond the "me" first selling approach of: "Get the salesperson to ask lots of questions, and then match our capabilities to what the client has said."

So, the sales force sits down and makes a list of questions designed to extract information from their prospective clients, in what amounts to, at least from the customer's perspective, an interrogation. I've sat through many sales calls like this, and trust me it's not only ineffective, it's also counterproductive.

To maximize the power of NeuroSelling we have to move beyond a simplistic view of consultative or even solution selling.

It's not about grilling the buyer but rather *engaging in a thought-provoking, trust-centered, customer-focused, problem-solving dialogue.*

One that focuses on the buyer's priorities, what's in their business's best interests, what prevents them from accomplishing what's in their best interest, and then helping them evaluate your solution against those challenges. Asking questions is part of this engagement process, but there's a right way and a wrong way to do this. Here are some important question-asking "potholes" to avoid in your customer conversations.

Stop the Traditional "Needs Analysis"

Recently, we began working with a financial services company that hadn't seen a ton of traction with their current sales approach. After observing a few client engagements, it was easy to see why. The sellers we observed did a decent job of asking lots of questions and getting back lots of answers, but it felt more like they were going through a checklist. Why? Because they were.

The dreaded "needs analysis" and, as a result, their sales calls felt mechanical, transactional, and self-focused.

While they did uncover some good information about clients' needs, allowing them to pivot and pitch the products they were selling, there was little buy-in from the prospects they were talking to and even less urgency to change.

There was no sense of empathy, shared interest, or that the client had confidence that the seller would be able to help them grow their business by solving specific problems that needed to be solved.

I've observed this scenario with both beginner and experienced salespeople, and, believe it or not, even senior executives of Fortune 500 clients. What we find is nearly always the same: when you focus primarily on questions *you* need the answer to in order to position your products or services, you rarely get the information you really need.

Start building a questioning strategy focused on the customer's objectives and challenges.

How do you do this?

Well, first you actually need to know your customer's objectives and challenges. "I know, Jeff...that's why we ask them so many questions...to learn those things. Duh."

You see, this is one of the fundamental mistakes being made in sales organizations across the globe today.

> You should never walk into a sales meeting until you have a strong understanding of the person or persons you are meeting with. What's their role? What does that role typically have as top five goals and objectives? How are they typically measured relative to those goals? What are the typical challenges or problems they face at accomplishing those goals that you solve for? If you can't answer those questions *before* you go to the meeting, you have no business going. The art of effective questions comes in learning more about the prospects feelings around these areas and creating questions that drive ownership of the problems by the prospect and an urgency to do something about it!

For example, if I call on financial advisors, I know that in general terms their top goals/objectives are:

A. Make more income

B. Gain more clients

C. Keep my current clients satisfied so they not only stay with me but also refer me to their friends

D. Simplify my business so I can have more balance in my life.

If you work in or around the financial services industry, you'll be hard pressed to find an advisor worth their weight who doesn't have these as top priorities.

Next, what problems or challenges do they face at accomplishing these goals that you solve for? Once you know these, you are armed with the right information to ask more laser-focused, customer-centric questions.

> **Bad question example:** *"Mrs. Advisor, how do you feel about using annuities to supplement your client's retirement strategy?"*
>
> **Great question example:** *"Mrs. Advisor, I recently read a survey that stated during the last market downturn, 40 percent of clients who left their advisor and went to a new advisor did so because they felt their current advisor didn't do enough to protect their assets. Obviously, when a client leaves you it not only hurts your income, but it also reduces your referrals. The right annuity positioned the right way has proven to be one of the most effective hedges against the dreaded market correction. How do you use annuities in your client's retirement strategy?"*

Don't miss this.

The difference is that *in the first question,* I ask a self-focused, product-driven question to learn information so I can tell you why you should use my product, in this case, an annuity, more often. All about me.

In the second question, I framed it around two specific problems to two specific goals you have as an advisor. First, your goal of client retention and second, your goal of referrals. Subtly, I put both those goals at risk using an insight from an article that I read (and be ready to source that article on the spot). Now that I have your mind focused on your goals and then your problems, I land a question that should evoke a more limbic-centered, emotional response.

The difference here is I didn't show up to a meeting with a list of "needs analysis" interrogation questions that only benefit me. **I showed up with a really good understanding of your world and then began a strategy of weaving in questions that are emotional and thought provoking around areas that you already care about.**

This approach takes a different mind-set and a willingness to learn and understand as much about your customer as you do about your product or solution. If you take the time to do this, you will never use a traditional needs analysis again.

Stop Asking Self-centered, Leading Questions

Very few things drive change resistance from a prospect faster than a question that either Captain Obvious would ask—i.e. "If your line failed and it cost you $1 million, would that be a problem for your business?" (Yes, I've actually heard that question asked in front of a prospect) or a question that is quite noticeably about you i.e. "If I can show you how effective my software works, would you be interested in seeing it in action?" In other words, "If I could show you something interesting, would you be interested?"

The kinds of questions sales professionals are typically taught to ask tend to focus on drawing attention to client problems, "pain points," and other potential sources of disappointment or dissatisfaction all in an attempt so the client will then view your offerings as a solution. It is useful to explore the buyer's challenges, but when you ask a ridiculous question with an obvious answer such as, "What's the implication of data-center failure?" it usually backfires. It's counterproductive because buyers immediately put up their defenses and will be skeptical of the seller's intentions.

Remember: *their brain is in risk mitigation mode and not until they are sure you can be trusted are they open to how you may help them.*

These types of questions trigger my cortisol, engage my fight or flight mechanism, and cause me to retreat inwardly to my closest place of safety. In addition, these types of questions lead me to feel you believe I'm an idiot and have made incredibly dumb decisions to this point which has me in the predicament (in your mind) that I'm in. Of course, I'm going to go into defense mode...even if you're right.

Start asking empathetic, curiosity-focused questions that your prospect can clarify and quantify.

When you ask questions that demonstrate a genuine curiosity, empathy, and a desire to understand me and my situation or goals better, it activates a different pathway in my brain.

Instead of my analytical pathway that ends in skepticism, distrust, and an unwillingness to consider new ideas, these types of questions travel down my empathic pathway in my brain which activates interest, builds trust, and creates an openness to learn something new that can help me.

By this point in the book, you know the science well. The key to asking great questions is using the science as your foundation but using the "art" of communication as the vehicle.

Great questions are as much about how they are asked, when they are asked, and from whose perspective they are asked than anything else.

Bad question example: *"If one of your assembly lines went down unexpectedly, would that be a problem for you and your team?"*

Great question example: *"Typically, in your industry, when an assembly line goes down unexpectedly, research suggests it can cost anywhere between $1 to $2 million in lost production revenue per month. Have you had this situation happen here at your facility in the last year? Were you able to identify the root cause of the interruption?"*

Once again, the way I've asked the second-question example shows the prospect that I understand their world, I've done research into their issues and I understand the pressure they must feel to prevent unplanned maintenance. Also, I've asked a secondary question to uncover their perspective on the cause.

Yes, I asked a closed-ended question first. Why?

Because if I sell a solution that helps prevent unplanned downtime and they never have unplanned downtime guess what they don't have. That's right, a problem that I can't even solve.

Also, once they've told me it has happened and they tell me why they think it happened, it allows me to direct my next line of questions more appropriately.

Stop Triggering Negative Neurochemistry

In her article, "*The Neurochemistry of Positive Conversations,*" Judith Glaser highlights and reinforces much of the science you've been learning in this book. More specifically, she discusses behaviors that contribute to the negative/stress chemical, or "cortisol-producing," and positive/trust chemical "oxytocin-producing" reactions in others.

Among the behaviors that create significant negative impacts are being focused on convincing others and behaving like others don't understand.

Precisely the behaviors that give salespeople a stereotypical bad name. Behaviors like being too aggressive, not listening, and going on and on about their product or service.

Conversely, the behaviors that create a positive chemical reaction include being concerned about others (empathy), stimulating discussions with genuine curiosity, and painting a picture of mutual success (visual storytelling in the limbic system).

Folks who have had tremendous success with NeuroSelling apply these techniques in their discussions with prospects and clients to create a collaborative dynamic with positive outcomes.

As you might have imagined, the degree of trust I have with you will determine how much information I will give you based on the question you ask.

Without trust, I will always be hesitant to give you information that I feel you may use against me but if I *really* trust you on a personal level, then I feel safe with you. I feel less risk from answering your questions because I believe you actually care about me, we have a connection and, in the end, you are the type of person that will do what's right. This is why your Why Story is such a critical tool in your toolbox. It not only helps you connect faster, but it also allows you to ask deeper, more insightful questions in a way that gives you more information in order to help your customer more effectively.

For the remainder of this chapter, I won't bore you with a long list of the different types of questions from open-ended to closed to probing, etc.... etc.... etc.... Instead, I'd prefer to walk you through the types of questions that work really well within the construct of NeuroSelling and your five "P" stories, Personal, Prospect, Problem, Product/Solution, Proof.

NeuroSelling Narrative-Friendly Questions

In your **Personal "Why" story,** asking questions based on how the other person "feels" about their beliefs, their sage, their purpose can be very powerful.

What I have found is wrapping your story and bridging like this seems to work well, *"So that's why I do what I do. How about you? Why do you do what you do?"*

Notice I didn't ask them about their resume or their experience. I ask them about their "why". This forces them to think differently about the question and about the story you just told them. As they begin to open up to you about their personal story, ask them questions along the way to demonstrate empathy and understanding.

"Your dad seemed like an incredible guy. If he were still here, what do you think he'd say he's most proud of you for?" or *"Wow, that's an incredible story. How do you think the beliefs your mom taught you have helped you be so successful in your career?"* These are simple questions, but they drive oxytocin and reinforce trust.

Once you move into the **Prospect story,** this is where you can begin a strategy of insightful, multilayered questions.

It's important to give your prospect an agreed-upon target first. We can use the one covered earlier in this chapter, *"In my experience, most financial advisors I work with are looking to attract new clients, keep their existing clients happy, and grow their revenue/income while simplifying their processes. Are those your top goals as well or would you add or subtract from that list?"*

Again, simple question but it's based on an anchor point of goals that I know later I can use my **Problem story** to put at risk if they don't change. From a multilayered questioning approach, you then drill down further. *"When it comes to attracting new clients, what has been your best strategy? What has been the most difficult aspect of gaining new clients?"*

Notice that I ask him a "success" question first. I want him to tell me what he thinks he's good at, *then* I ask him what he struggles with. I can continue this multilayered questioning approach until I feel he's expressed his thoughts and feelings around the goals he's actually trying to accomplish.

Next, in my Problem story, I will introduce the problem in a unique way. Maybe it's an analogy or metaphor or maybe it's a traditional story. Either way, it will end in a provocative question. Using third-party insight to position your Problem story is quite effective.

For example, if I told the prospect a story about a time I went mountain climbing without a guide and did it "free solo" with no anchors or ropes to protect me, I'll certainly have his attention. Then, when I tell him I almost fell a hundred feet to my death, he'll be hanging on every word.

> *"You know, it really reminds me of the fear investors have of an inevitable stock market correction. Free solo is the fastest way up a mountain...kind of like investing in traditional vehicles like stocks and mutual funds can be the fastest way to great returns in a great bull market. The problem is, when the wind picks up and the storm comes, if you're doing "free solo"-type investing only, it's also the fastest way down the mountain. For your clients, if you have all their money tied up in the market and the inevitable market correction hits, what's going to stop their fall? According to a survey by "XYZ" research firm, 75 percent of retirement-aged investors not only said they fear a market correction, but they also fear it will prevent them from living the retirement they had planned. "What is your current strategy to protect your clients from this type of inevitable fall?"*

You may feel like, "Man, Jeff...that sure seems like a long way around asking such a simple question."

Yes...and no. By building urgency with the story, you are able to relate the analogy of the free solo "risky" approach without the prospect knowing that's where you were going. *It drives curiosity and intrigue.*

Then, when you layer in the insight (75 percent of their clients say...) you create urgency around the problem. Now, when I ask him what his strategy is to protect his clients, it's **much more visual, personal, and urgent.** From there you can ask more multilayered questions to help uncover his true strategy and how you may be able to help him.

When you do finally pivot to introduce your **Product/Solution story,** you should start with a great question that begins to tie everything together. *"What if you could offer your prospects something so unique that it not only drove more business but also increased your referrals as well?"* Of course, the answer is "that would be awesome!" This may sound like a "Captain Obvious" question but it's actually tied directly to their main goals and objectives and is generally rhetorical in nature.

Then you tell your Product/Solution story in a way that ties directly back to how it solves the problems they agreed they had earlier in your conversation.

The questions from there should revolve around ensuring the prospect sees and understands the "value" of your solution. "If you began using my recommended strategy (Product/Solution), how do you feel it will help you in both the short and long run?" "Do you believe it will be easy to quantify the value?"

When it comes to asking effective "neurocentric" questions, it takes a great deal of awareness, practice, and preparation. You can't just go to "sales training" for a few days and gain mastery of this skill set, any more than you can jump on a flight simulator and within a week be able to land an Airbus A320 in the Hudson River like Captain Sully did back in 2009. Putting in the time to craft this type of questioning strategy will go a long way to driving empathy, trust, and an urgency to change on the part of your prospects.

REMOVING THE BARRIERS
TO CHANGE

*"People who appear to be resisting change
may simply be the victim of bad habits. Habit,
like gravity, never takes a day off."*

—Paul Gibbons, The Science of Successful Organizational Culture

TOM AND HIS wife had already bought the tickets. They'd been planning on a date night out to this show for weeks. At the last minute, though, something came up. You know how that goes.

They offered the tickets to Craig and his wife, Stacey, who they knew not only couldn't afford them, but who also could really use a night out. No charge, of course. If they couldn't enjoy the performance, they wanted their good friends to have a chance to get away and spend some quality time together.

"Gee, Tom, that sounds great! When is it?" Craig asked.

"This Saturday, seven o'clock," he replied.

"Oh, *this* Saturday? Man, I don't know. I mean, it's all the way downtown so an hour there, three hours for the show, an hour home, I don't know if we could get someone to watch the kids. Let's see, we'd also need to leave early to have dinner..."

On the one hand, Tom wanted to be aggravated. He'd spent a few hundred bucks for these tickets. He could easily go sell them on Facebook in a heartbeat. But he and his wife really wanted to do something nice for their friends. To be honest, he was already slightly annoyed that they themselves couldn't go, but then to have someone they were trying to help start talking about not knowing if they could go because they might need a babysitter or it might be too far away—I mean, did Craig not see that this was the perfect solution to the stress he and his wife were under?

The Moment of Change Resistance

Maybe you've been in a similar situation. Tom's emotional brain was at work. He told himself to calm down and let his neocortex kick in. His friend wasn't necessarily signaling indecision. It did seem he and his wife really wanted to go. He was likely just thinking out loud about all the things that had to fall into place in order to make it happen.

When it comes to our customer conversations, we tend to feel like we have the perfect solution for our customer's issues. Like Tom, we know Craig and Stacey need this night out (our solution) and can't for the life of us understand why he doesn't jump at the chance to implement it, right? Sometimes, the customer "Craigs" of the world just need more information to justify. Other times, there may be some hidden information we aren't aware of causing him to hesitate. Either way, it can feel frustrating but how we respond can make the difference between deepening the trust we have with the customer versus pushing them further into indecision.

If you've used NeuroSelling as the basis for your sales conversations, you'll be head and shoulders above "the other guys" who continue to fall back on their traditional sales techniques as they stay inside their safety box.

But what happens when you have that moment of change resistance? Traditional sales training often refers to this moment as an objection, but an objection by definition is a feeling of disapproval or opposition. If you've sold through old school means by asking a ton of leading questions then dumping all your "watches" out on the table to convince someone to buy, then yes, you likely get "objections."

> In the world of NeuroSelling, however, you establish personal trust up front, gain alignment and agreement on your customer's goals and objectives, then spend the rest of your time discussing the possible issues or problems that might prevent your customer from doing what they already told you they wanted to do!

When you then show them how you can help them prevent or solve those problems with your solution, why would they respond with disapproval or opposition to something they already told you they want help with?

Now, that's not to say they won't still have some anxiety around leaving their safety box. It's just coming from a much different place. In many cases, they are verbalizing the "barriers" to change they have to address in order to implement your solution. In the world of neuroscience, it's their neocortex now trying to ensure they can justify taking action on how they already feel. **They are looking for ways to say "yes" versus challenging you with an adversarial position of why they are saying "no."** In other words, NeuroSelling experts don't "overcome objections," they help the customer identify and remove any remaining barriers to change.

Let's take a different approach to Tom's situation. He and his wife knew that their friends had been struggling a bit. His friend's job situation was not the best. They had expressed challenges with their finances and everything was really beginning to put a strain on their relationship. (In other words, Tom really knew his customer and the customer's situation well.) What if Tom had taken this approach:

"Hey, how are you and Stacey doing?"

"Well, things are pretty rough right now. You know my job stress and that's putting strain on our finances and Stacey and I haven't been on a date in over three months."

"Sorry to hear that. We'd like to help. Do you remember telling me that your girls would love for our daughter, Sophie, to come babysit them again?"

"Yes, of course. They love her and so do we!"

"Well, how about this Saturday night? And...I'm going to do you one better: We have tickets for you and Stacey to the theater downtown. Seven o'clock show. Sophie cleared her calendar and can be to your house by three. That will give you both plenty of time to make it downtown, have a nice dinner, and see a great show."

You see, in many cases, when you know your "customer" well and understand their problem, you can position your "solution" in a way that alleviates many of the change barriers in the presentation of the solution itself. How could Tom's friend say "no" at this point?

The key is to think ahead and then be alright with your customer "processing" some of their fears or lingering barriers to saying yes. How you respond is critical. You have to respond in a way that shows your customer you are still on their agenda...caring about what they care about. That mind-set will help you process those emotions in a more constructive way when you perceive a barrier to change.

Let's take a look at some common ways to do just that....

Override Your Instincts

First, don't react the way Tom did initially.

Don't let your emotional brain start screeching. He was already frustrated, and for a moment he felt like his friend was being either ungrateful or blind to his own problem, which only added fuel to the fire. Tom made the horrible mistake of making the perceived barrier to change about him, not them.

When a customer starts voicing their worries or the obstacles, most salespeople's instinct is to retreat to their safety boxes. For most traditionally trained salespeople, that means using facts to tell the customer why they're wrong to feel the way they feel. Seeing the customer's hesitation spikes our cortisol: *Oh, no! They're not going to buy! I'm not going to make quota! I've got to make this sale! Yep. Self-preservation at its finest.*

Don't let the biology and physiology work against you.

Overcoming barriers to change isn't about responding emotionally as a sales representative, though that will be your instinct. *Your instinct will be to pull out your facts and try to club your customer over the head with all the reasons why they're wrong.* That's the last thing you want to do.

What you want to do is uncover the motives and the emotions behind the resistance and then reframe the discussion back to their goals and objectives they stated earlier in the conversation.

Let's say Tom's friend still hesitated even after the second approach. Asking a simple question may help reframe his friend back to the problem at hand.

"Listen, you and Stacey have been under tremendous stress. You told me yourself you've been neglecting your relationship for weeks if not months. This sure would go a long way in showing her how much she still means to you. That she's still a priority."

Yes, that's straight to the heart. But it's straight to the heart of the problem! Now, Tom's friend has to reconcile whether or not his relationship is a priority and if the lack of connection he and Stacey have been feeling is a real problem or not. I know, I'm using a nonselling example to illustrate the point. But my guess is, you get the point. Back to the customer...

Remember: *change barriers are emotional on the part of the customer.*

It's their root brain and their limbic system firing off into the self-preservation mechanism. It's trying to reduce risk. It's trying to minimize making a bad decision. So, by understanding this and following through this process, you'll be able to identify the "why" behind the resistance.

Second, what you're hearing as resistance may just be their neo-cortex speaking up. Don't be afraid when you see your customer start to do this. It could very well mean that they've already made a decision and just need additional information to plug the gaps. Even if it is a genuine barrier, it at least means the customer hasn't dismissed your solution out of hand. They're processing what it would look like to move forward.

Third, it's important to reflect on their barrier relative to where your conversation may have missed the mark. After working as a salesperson, sales manager, and sales and marketing executive for most of my career, I can tell you that when buyers don't make a decision to change, it's usually due to one or more of the following reasons:

1. **Lack of trust** – this one hurts because it's personal. You likely failed to make the necessary connection. Way to go, lack of differentiated, commoditized bottle of water with a different label salesperson.

2. **Lack of urgency** – usually due to you not positioning the problem appropriately or quantifying the cost of status quo.

3. **Lack of budget** – this can be real but can also be a smokescreen. If the problem you're solving either helps save money or make money in a tangible way, most buyers will find the money to pay for it.

4. **Don't see the value** – In this case, they don't believe the price of your solution is worth more than what they might save or gain by purchasing it.

5. **Don't believe your claims** – this ultimately comes down to trust but, in this case, they simply don't believe your solution will do what you say it will do. Therefore, they don't see it as a solution to a problem.

6. **Don't feel the timing is right** – similar to lack of urgency, sometimes a buyer will tell you they love everything about your solution

but have to wait until things "calm down," etc... etc.... This simply means they don't see the urgency to solve this specific problem today; therefore you likely missed out on an opportunity to quantify the problem somewhere along the conversation.

Do any of these sound familiar to you? How do your customers express these differently?

Knowing this brings us to our fourth point—understand that you already have the tools to address any one of these barriers to change.

Your Why Story should create connection and trust...if you use it.

As you've read, even delivered imperfectly, it's still amazingly effective. **Remember:** *personal trust is the key to the rest of the conversation.*

If they don't trust you, they're never going to tell you that the real reason they don't want to move forward is because they're in the doghouse with their boss right now, or that they're embarrassed that the last "solution" totally bombed.

With the other five reasons, you need to go back to your "P" narratives (prospect, problem, product, proof). If they don't feel the urgency or that the timing is right, it probably means you didn't quantify the gap. If you've properly framed the problem as a $4 million-per-production-line problem, I'll bet they could probably find the money in a capital expenditures budget. If they don't feel the need, then you didn't identify the right issue/problem in the first place.

Here's how I might reframe their barrier:

> *Mr. Customer, I must have misunderstood something from our earlier conversation. You mentioned that your primary problem right now is to reduce the overall energy footprint of your business while at the same time saving $1 million per year in direct energy costs. What different options are you looking at to accomplish that goal?*

I mean, I'd be genuinely confused.

Next, I'd like to introduce you to a tool that will help you identify and remove change-resistance barriers.

As mentioned, **a change barrier is always rooted in emotion.** That emotion is centered around the relationship a customer feels between their perception of risk versus the perception of value. For all my math friends out there, it's a pretty simple set of equations. **The depth of the barrier is equal to the level of risk perceived compared to the perception of overall value:**

$$Barrier = Risk > Value$$

$$Change = Value > Risk$$

Once you've identified the change barrier, you can begin to ask insightful questions to uncover the root emotions associated with the barrier and then begin to subtly quantify those emotions relative to the customer's perception of risk compared to their belief in the value of your solution.

Let's look at a few examples. You go all the way through your customer conversation with precision but in the end, your prospect begins to ask a lot of questions around your price. You can tell they think you are too expensive. This is obviously a pretty common barrier.

In this example, let's say you sell a top-of-the-line, manufacturing automation software that allows companies to streamline their production which increases throughput, decreases downtime, and does so with the least possible energy consumption on the market. In your conversation, the customer gave you their current problem areas with throughput, downtime, and energy consumption. You were able to quantify those "problem" areas that totaled around $4 million annually. Your solution will cost around $1 million to implement. Let's now look at the customer's resistance barrier through the equation.

What's the emotion here? It's always rooted in fear, but fear of what? What's the risk in their mind?

For starters, your solution will require a significant amount of training for their floor managers and IT department. Next, it will require a complete change in the way the customer moves inventory and raw materials to the lines. In other words, they will have to change their internal processes. These changes alone create a significant amount of anxiety for your prospect.

On a scale of 1–10, I would put them at an 8 in terms of level of risk perception. On the value scale, they see your $1 million price tag and compare that to two things: 1. The cost of doing nothing and, 2. The cost of simply upgrading their current technology which, though not as advanced as your solution, will only cost them $500,000. In their mind, they would likely put the "value" score of your solution at a 4 on a 1–10 scale.

In our equation, the "R" is clearly greater than the "V."

This means your customer's emotional change-resistance barrier score is a 2. Anything over a 1 usually means no deal. Yes, this is a subjective score, but it gives you an internal compass to direct your conversation.

So what can you do?

Ask insightful questions tied back to your earlier conversation.

"Mr. Customer, earlier you expressed to me that, as a company, you had a handful of critical goals. One of those goals was to cut production costs by 20 percent across the board. The other was to reduce your overall energy footprint by 40 percent in the spirit of the "green" initiative. Let's look at both of those goals again individually.

On the production cost-cutting front, how will doing nothing or upgrading your current technology impact that goal? Production costs are really a factor of output versus time, correct?

"Yes".

With your current system, even if you upgraded it to the maximum available technology, it reduces downtime by 10 percent but doesn't actually increase overall output proportionally. From a very practical standpoint, you can invest $500K on those upgrades and reduce your problem of $4 million down to $3.6 million.

So, I suppose you could say that reduces your production cost, but does it actually meet the goal? With our solution, you invest $1 million and you actually eliminate unplanned downtime entirely while at the same time increase output by 20 percent due to the efficiency of the automation.

So not only do you go from a $4 million problem to zero, but you also actually increase your production from $20 million per line per day to $24 million per line per day. That seems like quite a difference. Do you agree with my math?"

From there, you can tackle their barrier around fear of internal processes having to change.

"Mr. Customer, you also expressed concern over how your internal processes will have to change to implement this solution. I can certainly understand that fear. Typically, the real concern our customers have is around the direct impact to productivity during the implementation as well as the personnel impact to your team. Does that appropriately describe your concern?

"Yes".

Well, the good news is, we have mastered the implementation process. We have an entire team of implementation specialists who work directly with your team to design and execute the changeover plan one line at a time. Because you don't run every line 24/7, our team works to implement our solution during the off-peak, normal slow times when you already have lines nonoperational. If that means we are in there from midnight to 6:00 a.m., then so be it.

The point is, you won't experience production interruption and your current team will be a part of the solution from day one, so there will be significant buy-in. Does this address your concerns around both the value and the potential fear of "pain of change" in the implementation?"

Here's the key to any barrier to change. You have to identify the barrier. Identify the emotion behind the barrier. Understand the prospect's perception of risk compared to the perception of value and then use the information you should have already uncovered in your NeuroSelling conversation to help alleviate their concern and reduce their cortisol.

It's important to remember, the customer has anchor points that they (and hopefully you), have been setting all along your conversation. If you're executing the NeuroSelling model correctly, you've been setting some of those anchors relative to the cost of the problem.

So, by resetting the anchor point back to the cost of the problem—and, most importantly, the cost of doing nothing—you can go back to the opportunity and remind them what their initial goals were to begin with. Then you can go back to showing them how your solution solves that problem and all the reasons why they want to say yes.

It's taking the barrier and reframing that obstacle as the opportunity that answers or accomplishes the customer's objective.

The brain associates value based on contrast. If I don't believe my problem is worth X and you're charging Y, I'm never going to pay what you're asking for. If the barrier is price, you haven't been able to create enough value between the cost of the problem and the price you're charging. Now that could be on you, it could be on your conversation with the customer, it could be on your pricing model. More than likely it's on you as a sales representative. You haven't done a thorough enough job creating the contrast in the customer conversation.

If, at the end of the conversation, I give my solution and then the price, and the customer says, "Whew! That much? I just don't think I'm going to be able to swing that. That seems steep..."

When that happens, I just look at the information we'd been working off of the entire conversation and say, "Well, let me just make sure I understand what you said earlier. We're trying to solve a $4 million problem. Do you feel like that's accurate?" Now, they should, because they're the one who said it.

"So, what you're telling me is that is you don't believe the $1 million investment in my engineering solution will solve that $4 million problem?"

By asking them that question, you will uncover their true motives for their barrier.

If they don't really believe that to be true, if they don't believe your solution is as good as you think it is, it isn't about the price. It's that they don't believe your solution will solve the problem. Then you can have an entirely different conversation around capabilities.

Always keep in mind. Barriers to change are emotional in nature. They are tied to a set of anchor points your customer has that are likely not the anchors you want them to have. Reset those anchors, reduce the risk, and reestablish the value of your solution relative to the problem. Reset, Reduce, Reestablish.

Say it with me: "Reset, Reduce, Reestablish."
Now you are ready to tackle any barrier to change!

CLOSING VS. COMMITTING

"You can have everything in life that you want if you will just help enough other people get what they want."
—Zig Ziglar

ONE OF THE most memorable times in a sales meeting went like this: I'd made a real connection with the VP of Sales. He wanted to roll out NeuroSelling for his whole team. Of course, he needed the CEO's backing. So, he'd gotten all the executives into the boardroom and asked me to "tell our story" again.

I started out with my same "my why" Papaw story I'd shared with the VP and then moved my new audience systematically through the NeuroSelling model. It didn't take long until we got into the real problem: They needed to increase sales by 20 percent to hit their revenue goals.

"How much would a 20 percent increase represent in real dollars?"

The CEO answered, "A hundred million dollars."

"And how many salespeople do you have?"

"A hundred," the sales VP answered.

"So, you really have a million dollar-per-rep problem, don't you?" I said.

We continued to talk about NeuroSelling, the science behind effective communication, and what Braintrust had done for others.

After about forty-five minutes of great whiteboarding and questions going back and forth, the CEO stood up and said, "Jeff, this sounds exactly like what we need. Let's get it on the books!" He shook my hand and then walked out the door.

"Hey!" I called after him. "Don't you care how much it costs?!"

He poked his head back in room and laughed. "Sure! How much does it cost?"

"Well, you have a $1 million-per-rep problem, right? How much is it worth to you to solve it?"

He laughed again and walked back out.

Over his shoulder, he yelled, "Teach my team how to negotiate like you! Send me the bill!"

I mean, right there, in front of all his VPs, he'd basically just given me a blank check. Of course, we took them through the same program at our standard rate, but think about it: What a world of difference to go from defending your value and competing on price to the customer dying laughing and not even worried about getting the best price?

Once you know how big the problem is—and the cost of inaction—then the solution that you eventually propose should look like a bargain by comparison.

If they have a $1 million-per-rep problem...how much would they be willing to spend to solve that problem?

NeuroSelling salespeople don't close.

You've probably been taught one of two sales methods: either the hard close (yuck!) or to wait for the customer to ask for a contract (yawn...). Neither is an option in NeuroSelling.

Gong, a big, data analytics sales research firm has now used their technology to analyze over a million sales conversations. They set out to determine the trends and favorable characteristics that lead to new business. Guess what they found? *Closing techniques are not only ineffective, but they also actually cause you to sell less.* In fact, they found that the best way to positively impact the *end* of your customer conversations is to change the *beginning!*

Chris Orlob, Director of Sales at Gong.io, uses a great analogy to explain their research findings. Imagine an asteroid that has already entered the earth's atmosphere. Changing its course at that point (toward the end of the journey) will have little effect on the overall catastrophic impact. However, when the asteroid is all the way back at the beginning of its journey, even a slight modification to its path will bring about substantial changes to the overall trajectory of the journey and, hence, the outcome.

So it is with your customer conversations as well. Trying to "correct" or change closing techniques is a waste of your time. Improving your skills earlier in the customer conversation, as we've been discussing this entire book, will yield far greater results for the end of the journey.

Great salespeople don't close. They lead the customer to a natural, logical "choice" to solve their problem with your solution!

Just like with that CEO laughing his way out of the room: I didn't have to close him. I didn't *need* to close him. If I have built great personal and professional trust and forged a great partnership with someone, working together just seems like the right thing to do. The smart thing to do.

If you've earned their personal and professional trust and let them come to the decision themselves, then you have earned the right to ask for their commitment but that "ask" can't be your typical closing questions. You must transfer the power...the choice back to the prospect at that point. It has to be their choice.

This could begin with something like:

> *"Mr. Customer, based on the conversation we've had today, it's clear that solving these issues together will be mutually beneficial.*

We will have a great deal of time, money, and resources invested in delivering this solution, as will you and your company, but I believe it will be worth the effort on both of our parts."

Obviously, this is the windup to the pitch. You're setting them up for the sale.

But then...

The Million-Dollar Question

This one question is so important that I've devoted an entire subheading to it. I call it the million-dollar question because it's a million-dollar idea that's made our team and our clients millions of dollars over the past decade. Drumroll, please...here's the question:

"What would you like to do?"

Don't miss the power in the simplicity of that question.

When our children were younger and we were trying to instill independence, we would lay out two options. "We can wait until Sunday morning to lay our clothes out for church. Or, we can lay our clothes out tonight, leave earlier, and have enough time to go get doughnuts. What would *you* like to do?"

Of course, they wanted to get doughnuts. They willingly and cheerfully got their clothes out. We didn't have to tell them to. We didn't have to sell them on the idea. They saw the options and chose to do it themselves.

And if you think that we adults aren't just big kids, think back to the last time someone ordered you to do something. "Well, isn't that what you were going to do anyway?" "Yeah, but I didn't need *him* to tell me that!" We don't like having decisions forced upon us.

You can't order your customer to buy from you, but the psychology is the same. If you tell them, "Okay, here's what we need to do to move forward," then you've taken that choice away. You're making the decision for them. Nobody likes that, no matter how old they are.

On the other hand, if you never ask for their business, then you never give them a chance to say yes. I once heard someone say, "If you give a customer all the time in the world, they'll take it." If they don't know that it's time to take action—if you don't ask for some sort of commitment—then how are they supposed to know?

Simply ask: "What would you like to do?"

Gaining Commitment

NeuroSelling devotees don't close.

We gain commitment.

Like everything else you've read in this book, I hope you understand that this is deeper than semantics.

At the end of Step Four when you're presenting your solution and tying it back to the problem, we don't believe in the cheesy, "So, what's it going to take to get you to say yes today, Mr. Customer?" nonsensical question because we know that doesn't work.

"If you've done the homework, the test is easy." If you've established connection and credibility and followed the rest of NeuroSelling, then this step should almost take care of itself.

I recommend saying something like, "Mr. Customer, based on the conversation we've had today, the problem you're experiencing and how much it's actually costing you, it seems like our solution is the perfect fit. So, what would you like to do?"

Now, that may seem like a completely simple and innocuous question, but it's powerful in its Neuroscience capabilities. Because remember those cognitive biases? When I say, "What would you like to do?" I am giving you the power. You have the choice to take ownership. I'm allowing you to confirm, using your own confirmation and choice-supportive bias in my favor. I'm also allowing you to take the opportunity to jump on the bandwagon and join the other customers who've felt the same way that we want you to feel by saying yes.

I'm putting all the power over to you, but I'm not allowing you to not make a choice. So, by saying, "What would you like to do?" you have to respond with some form of action. How you respond to that form of action will tell me exactly where I stand in relation to getting this deal done.

If you say you'd like to take time to think about it, then I know that I haven't closed the gap. I know that I haven't presented something somewhere along the conversation in a way that is going to drive urgency to change. Great sales representatives don't like to leave a sales conversation with a maybe. I'd much rather you tell me no and the reasons why or tell me yes. But "maybe" is never an option for me.

If I think if I've done everything correctly in the first five steps of our model, I've earned the right to get an honest yes or no.

This is what we call the power of the "partnership agreement."

"Mr. Customer, in order for us to implement this solution, you know, we have a lot of time, people, energy, and resources invested in bringing this solution to you, just like you're going to have a lot of time, resources, and energy invested in us solving this problem with our solution. So, collectively, we've got a lot at stake joining together to solve this problem."

Language like this goes a long way to helping create a partnership model in the mind of the customer. Sometimes they forget that you have a lot at stake at solving this problem. Sometimes they forget that you have a lot of energy and time and money and resources invested in helping bring this solution to them. *Just by simply stating that with empathy and humility, you remind their subconscious part of their brain that they trust you, feel a connection to you, and this is a win/win solution.*

For Access to Free Bonus Tools to Help You Implement
the Concepts of NeuroSelling, go to:

www.braintrustgrowth.com/neurosellingtools

APPENDIX: NEUROSELLING JUMP START

IT'S TAKEN ME a lifetime to put the pieces of NeuroSelling together. I hope it saves you years of learning, helps increase your sales dramatically, and enables you to help far more customers. Most importantly, I hope it helps you be a more impactful communicator in every area of your life. However, just like your prospects, you have to *choose* to implement the information contained within these pages.

I understand this book contains a lot of information. It can be hard to absorb it all in one setting. It some ways, it can feel like I've held a fire-hose a few feet from your face and pulled the lever. Even our clients who attend our full workshops feel a bit overwhelmed at first. After all, I am asking you not only to leave your existing safety box, but I'm also giving you a scientific rationale as to why. Your fear of change coupled with your potential fear of not being able to execute each piece of this approach can be a challenge. My guess is that many of you recognize areas covered in this book as concepts you've been doing well but possibly didn't know the reason why they worked. For other areas, maybe the concepts here help reveal places in your customer conversation that can still improve.

As a way to "bring it all together" in one place, you may find the following road map or "cheat sheet" helpful. After reading all this, you may be looking for a "cheat sheet" to help you get started. I've got you covered!

#1. People buy from people they trust. There are two types of trust, personal and professional. Not until your prospect trusts you personally will they drop their self-preservation shield in order to see how you may help them professionally. Feelings of trustworthiness drive up oxytocin, the "trust" neurochemical. The quickest way to do this is with the first of your "P" narratives, your PERSONAL "why" story.

#2. Your prospect needs to see that you understand their world. Instead of asking a hundred "probing" questions, present them with three to five typical goals or objectives someone in their role tends to focus on by utilizing the second "P" narrative, the PROSPECT story. Then, ask questions about their perspective around those goals. This allows you to not only discuss areas they care about, but it also allows you to give them a "menu" to choose from as opposed to asking blind "what are you struggling" with questions that could lead you down a rabbit trail that you didn't intend to go.

#3. Once you've established the prospects goals, you have to effectively introduce narrative #3, the PROBLEM story. This will be the villain that prevents your hero (prospect) from accomplishing their mission (goals). This problem story should be what puts their current status quo at risk. It should speak directly to what could prevent them from accomplishing the goals discussed in the prospect narrative. In addition, you should ensure you "quantify" the problem(s). This gives you the anchor to the cost of the problem that you will want the prospect to compare to later versus the price of your solution. Failure to quantify the problem is a common, but costly mistake. Don't make it.

#4. Now that you've connected with your personal "why" story, gained alignment on their goals in the prospect story, positioned the problem

story as the barrier to accomplishing those goals and quantified the cost of either the problem or status quo, it's time for the **PRODUCT/ SOLUTION** story. Finally, it's your time to solve the problem with your solution. The difference now is, however, that your solution actually looks like a solution since it's solving an actual problem compared to simply features and benefits to a product that I really don't care about. Make sure when you present your product/solution story that you explain specifically and simply how it solves the problem you've been discussing.

#5. Next, you simply need to allow their neocortex to validate and justify the positive way they feel about your solution with your PROOF story. This story contains the evidence that what you are claiming is true and how other customers have solved the same or similar problems with your solution as well.

#6. When it comes to change, keep in mind that the brain has to work through several barriers, even when it feels good about potentially moving forward. Evaluate your prospect's change barriers through the emotional lens of risk divided by value perception. Ensure you empathize with the concerns they may have from a "risk" standpoint. Address as many of those concerns during your actual product/solution story, if possible, as that may help alleviate the concerns around those barriers before they ever become barriers. Empathetically helping a prospect work through the emotion associated with the perception of risk to them and their organization will go a long way in cementing trust and getting to "yes."

#7. Don't close. Create an environment of trust and change the customer conversation at the *beginning* instead of trying to improve your "closing" skills. We know that people choose to buy. Nobody ever wants to be sold. Allow your customer to "choose" your solution as the logical choice to solving their problem. Create a partnership agreement and then hit them with that million-dollar, cognitive-bias-driven commitment question, "What would you like to do?" You've earned the right to ask for a commitment and they feel they are in control of making that commitment. You both win. More often.

Keep in mind, each step in this road map as well as all the suggestions throughout this book are based on the biology, psychology, and physiology of decision-making. The science is the reason to change. The science gives you a new "anchor" from which to begin a different type of customer conversation.

In the end, sales isn't about selling.

It's about serving your customers by solving their problems.

That mind-set shift will go a long, long way to allowing your prospects and customers to actually believe you care about them. Because you do. In fact, I'll be so bold as to suggest it's even "why" you do what you do. And when you live from your place of "why," your "what" becomes more relevant and your "how" becomes more easily executed and your purpose becomes even more evident. Now go change the world, one problem at a time!

For Access to Free Bonus Tools to Help You Implement
the Concepts of NeuroSelling, go to:

www.braintrustgrowth.com/neurosellingtools

ENDNOTES

CHAPTER 1

[1]http://www.loc.gov/loc/brain/emotion/Ledoux.html
[2]http://webhome.auburn.edu/~mitrege/ENGL2210/USNWR-mind.html

CHAPTER 3

[1]Daniel Kahneman's groundbreaking book *Thinking, Fast and Slow* does an excellent job of explaining the science behind basic human decision-making.

CHAPTER 4

[1]https://www.amazon.com/Daring-Greatly-Courage-Vulnerable-Transforms/dp/1592408419
[2]https://journals.sagepub.com/doi/abs/10.1111/j.1467-9280.2007.02010.x
[3]https://www.tandfonline.com/doi/abs/10.3109/10673229.2011.549771
[4]https://www.sciencedirect.com/science/article/abs/pii/S0006322310001204
[5]https://www.ncbi.nlm.nih.gov/pmc/articles/PMC3582747/
[6]https://www.ncbi.nlm.nih.gov/pmc/articles/PMC5645535/
[7]YF Guzmán, Tronson NC, Jovasevic V, Sato K, Guedea AL, Mizukami H, Nishimori K, Radulovic J (September 2013). "Fear-enhancing effects of septal oxytocin receptors". Nature Neuroscience. 16 (9): 1185–7.
[8]https://www.ncbi.nlm.nih.gov/pubmed/15834840
[9]https://www.sciencedirect.com/science/article/pii/S0018506X09000853?via%3Dihub
[10]https://www.cell.com/neuron/fulltext/S0896-6273(08)00327-9?_returnURL=https%3A%2F%2Flinkinghub.elsevier.com%2Fretrieve%2Fpii%2FS0896627308003279%3Fshowall%3Dtrue
[11]https://www.amazon.com/Moral-Molecule-Source-Love-Prosperity/dp/0525952810
[12]https://www.amazon.com/Presence-Bringing-Boldest-Biggest-Challenges/dp/0316256579
[13]https://www.sciencedirect.com/science/article/pii/S0301051108002202
[14]https://www.annualreviews.org/doi/10.1146/annurev.neuro.27.070203.144230
[15]THE NEUROSCIENCE OF COACHING; Richard E. Boyatzis and Anthony I. Jack, Consulting Psychology Journal: Practice and Research, 2018, Vol. 70, No. 1, 11–27

CHAPTER 5

[1] https://www.amazon.com/ONE-Thing-Surprisingly-Extraordinary-Results/dp/1885167776

CHAPTER 6

[1] https://www.salesforce.com/blog/2015/11/7-signs-need-sales-enablement-solution.html
[2] https://books.google.com/books?id=m8qMjPF1NYAC
[3] https://gero.usc.edu/labs/matherlab/files/2019/03/HenkelMather2007.pdf
[4] https://onlinelibrary.wiley.com/doi/abs/10.1002/smj.3092

CHAPTER 7

[1] https://siteresources.worldbank.org/DEVMARKETPLACE/Resources/Handout_
TheLearningPyramid.pdf
[2] https://womensleadership.stanford.edu/stories
[3] https://www.ncbi.nlm.nih.gov/pmc/articles/PMC3269540/

CHAPTER 8

[1] https://hbr.org/2006/07/what-makes-a-good-salesman

For more information, visit us at: www.braintrustgrowth.com

For consulting inquiries to have NeuroSelling brought
to your organization: info@braintrustgrowth.com

To inquire about having me speak at your next event:
jeffbloomfield@braintrustgrowth.com